LOOK
UNTO
HIM

Published by Covenant Communications, Inc.
American Fork, Utah

Printed in China
First Printing: September 2022

27 26 25 24 23 22   10 9 8 7 6 5 4 3 2 1

ISBN 978-1-52442-237-0

JOHN BYTHEWAY, AL CARRAWAY,
JODY MOORE, HANK SMITH, ANTHONY SWEAT
ART BY EVA KOLEVA TIMOTHY

LOOK
UNTO
HIM

Finding the Love of Christ in Our Lives

Years ago, I came across a painting of Christ in a small makeshift chapel in Sofia, Bulgaria, that was so vastly different from the iconic art of Orthodoxy I'd grown up with that it left a profound impression on me. This series of sacred art, "The Lord Is My Light," was largely inspired by the awe I felt in that moment. It is not a strict recreation of scriptural scenes but an intimate view of the Savior's love for us as individuals.

Following a pre-Raphaelite notion of simplicity and sincerity, I often omit faces and tangential figures from the stories, leaving the focus on the act and sentiments surrounding the Lord's ministering.

It is my hope that those who view this collection of artwork will experience some of the same emotions I have felt in its creation as they look for and see more of the Lord's light and guiding hand in their lives.

This book is dedicated to my dear parents, Stefka and Lubomir, who taught me to always look for the light. Your love and faith have made all the difference.

—Eva Koleva Timothy

As a religious educator, I am consistently helping my students see what they are reading in the scriptures. I ask, "What does this story look like in your mind?" I'm fascinated by their answers as they attempt to describe the indescribable. The joy in this particular project was that Eva's art captures so much of what I see in my mind as I read the stories of the Savior's life.

The last few years haven't been what I'd hoped they'd be. No one saw a global pandemic coming, and I certainly didn't foresee my brother, a close family friend, and my father all passing away within ninety days of each other. The other authors of this book picked me up when I fell. I originally thought I'd do all the writing myself, but then life handed me a burden too heavy to bear alone. I called upon Jody, Al, Anthony, and John for help, and they came to my rescue. I will always cherish the four of them for carrying my burden over the finish line when I could not.

For those who view and read this beautiful volume, I hope you'll feel that same sense of strength from being part of a covenant community.

This book is dedicated to my assistant, Lisa Spice. It would never have seen the light of day without you.

—Hank Smith

TABLE OF CONTENTS

LOOK UNTO ME

Doctrine and Covenants 6:36

I recently had a confused student, whose faith was faltering, come to my office seeking some answers. Various tributaries of societal, cultural, gender, sexual, historical, and doctrinal issues had flowed together into an un-swimmable river in which her faith was drowning. Paraphrasing her concerns, she lamented: "Why would God allow this to happen? Why would He say this at one time and that at another time? How come this unfairness exists? Why didn't He stop this mistake from happening in the Church? Why would He allow this prophet to teach that? Why doesn't He reveal more on this?"

I tried to help her, but I didn't seem to be succeeding. Eventually, she broke down and sobbed, saying, "I'm so confused! I don't even know where to look anymore for answers."

When she said that, finally a clear answer came to me.

"I do," I said.

"Where?" she cried.

I opened my Doctrine and Covenants and read aloud, "Look unto me in every thought; doubt not, fear not" (Doctrine and Covenants 6:36).

She responded, "I don't think the answer is that simple."

"It's not simple, but I actually do think it is the clear answer," I said and then asked a pointed question. "Are you looking to the Savior and relying on His divine promises? Or are you looking to society and doubting and fearing?"

These few verses and our conversation, of course, didn't answer the student's important and pressing questions. More time, listening, study, dialogue, and patience is needed to continue to seek solutions to some of these

spiritually vexing issues in contemporary society. But I truly do believe within those verses is the directive on how to continue in our faith despite our spiritual struggles, whatever they may be.

When I look into the faces of so many good and capable people in the Church wherever I speak or teach—particularly its young people—I don't worry that the thing that will take them out of the restored gospel and away from their covenants with God are their sincere questions. Nor do I worry it is modern societal values (some of which are better aligned with the gospel than previous generations). Nor do I worry that what will derail them is their falling too much into sin.

What I worry about most is them listening too much to their *fears*.

Fear is a basic human emotion and, of course, a healthy level of fear is a good thing to keep us safe and well. I'm not talking about that danger-related fear. I'm talking about fear related to divine doubt—the kind that causes us to look away from God and turn from Him. I'm talking about fear that is the antithesis of faith. Faith is trust. Faith is confidence. Faith

FAITH
IS
TRUST.

LOOK UNTO ME

Doctrine and Covenants 6:36

I wanted to capture the tender way in which the Lord seeks to focus our eyes on Him. There are so many distractions that can draw our attention away from Christ and our real purpose here on Earth.

God knows that as we center our lives on Him and keep our eye single to His glory, our faith in Him and our power to accomplish all we came here to do will grow. Still, He doesn't force our perspective; rather, He addresses us in utter tenderness and allows us to make the decision to look unto Him in every thought.

impels to action. Faith is the source of divine power. Fear is the exact opposite. Fear doesn't know what to do, only what not to do. Fear closes its eyes, turns its head, and freezes. Fear forms protective padded walls all around us, defending against all possible failures and thus all possible success. Fear is the emotion of immobility. Thus, fear is a prison. Fear is damning. Fear is hell.

The scriptures are keen on this concept, telling us to "fear not" ninety-one times by my count. I don't know of many divine injunctions more often expressed than that command. In the very section of Doctrine and Covenants being discussed in this chapter—"Look unto me in every thought; doubt not, fear not" (Doctrine and Covenants 6:36)—the Lord says it two times preceding this verse: "Fear not to do good, my sons, for whatsoever ye sow, that shall ye also reap" (verse 33) and "Fear not, little flock; do good; let earth and hell combine against you" (verse 34). Then "doubt not, fear not" three times in a row. So what does Oliver Cowdery—to whom this section is directed—do with this triple reminder? He fears! And in the process he loses his opportunity to help translate the Book of Mormon: "It was expedient when you commenced: *but you feared*, and the time is past, and it is not expedient now" (Doctrine and Covenants 9:11; emphasis added).

The Lord rebuked a group of early elders who had been promised to be endowed with apostolic power and to rend the veil to see the face of God (but who mostly failed); He said, "Ye endeavored to believe that ye should receive the blessing which was offered unto you; but behold, verily I say unto you *there were fears in your hearts*, and verily this is the reason that ye did not receive" (Doctrine and Covenants 67:3; emphasis added).

When the winds of a storm on the Sea of Galilee threatened to sink the disciples' ship with the Lord on board, Jesus—almost bewildered—says, "Why are ye so fearful? How is it that ye have no faith?" Ironically, the very next line says, "And they feared exceedingly" (Mark 4:40–41). Sometimes we are no different. At least, I know I'm no different. With Jesus on board, we yet look at the storms and fear. There are days when the demands of my Church calling, the pressures of my work, the duties of being a father, and the responsibilities of a husband pile up on me, and I despair. Admittedly, sometimes I pay too much attention to the news, the chatter on social media, those who are critical of the Church, my own criticisms, and people who are

> Faith is the source of divine power. Fear is the exact opposite . . . a prison.

leaving the faith, and I feel the cold feeling of fear creep into the cracks of my foundation of faith, seeking to freeze and explode small fissures into large fractures.

What can we do when this happens? First, let us understand that God doesn't work through these feelings of fear. "For God hath not given us the spirit of fear; but of power, and of love, and of a sound mind" (2 Timothy 1:7). "Let us not take counsel from our fears," President James E. Faust once taught.[1] Being a

believer doesn't mean we won't have or experience fear. But being a faithful believer does mean we know where to tell our fears to get off so we can get on. I heard someone once say that fear may be along for the ride, but we should never let it drive. Especially, I would add, when it comes to faith.

Above all, we need to look to Christ, trust His divine promises, and "be not afraid, only believe" (Mark 5:36). Faith in Him, hope in His promises, and a surety that His "perfect love casteth out fear" (1 John 4:18) will lead to the "fountain of all righteousness" (Ether 12:28). Returning to the story of the student I began this chapter with and along these lines of faith in Christ and His divine promises to cast out all fear, I asked her things like:

"Are you looking to Christ, or are you looking away and doubting and fearing?"

"Do you believe that God is in charge and actively involved in guiding His Kingdom, Church, and children?"

"Do you believe He loves us, understands us, and wants to help us?"

"Do you believe the Lord will yet reveal many great and important things pertaining to the kingdom of God?"

---

1 James E. Faust, "Be Not Afraid," *Ensign*, October 2002, 6.

"Do you believe that He will help you and strengthen you in the challenges of mortality?"

"Do you believe that through the Savior's Atonement He can and will make all mortal wrongs right?"

"Do you believe the arc of the universe bends toward Restoration and that He will fully restore, and then some?"

As I asked her these things, I internally asked if I believed the same. If we don't believe these things, then we might feel as if we will drown in the overflowing river of mortal questions and concerns. But if we do believe, and believe all other things the Lord our God has promised, then we have every reason to "doubt not [and] fear not."

UNTO US A SON IS GIVEN; THE LORD IS WITH THEE

Luke 1:28

Create a picture in your mind of the ancient city of Ephesus. From a bird's-eye view you see what you'd describe as ancient Roman or Greek buildings lining a green hillside. From the hill above the city you can see the walls surrounding the city and the Aegean Sea off in the distance. Statues and columns line the stone-paved streets of the city. You see people walking to the market, emptying out of an open-air amphitheater, or collecting around the massive Temple of Artemis. Roman soldiers talk among themselves as they patrol the entrances to the city.

A younger man is walking down one of the smaller neighborhood streets on the outskirts of the city. Each street has roads leading to common areas that are surrounded by stone apartments. Children are playing in these common areas while men and women are mending clothes, binding fence posts together, or braiding crowns of fresh flowers. Animals are tied close to the front entrances of each apartment. The man is polite as he walks, occasionally stopping to ask if he can find the home of the one they call John the Apostle. He finally walks toward the door he has been directed to. Taking a deep breath, he calls to anyone in the two-story apartment. *"Khaíre?"* he calls. "Hello?"

An older woman turns in her chair. Her gray hair reflects the light from the door. *"Hypíaine,"* she responds. "Good morning."

The young man tells the woman his name is Luke and he is seeking the one called John, the Apostle of Jesus Christ. He has come to Ephesus, he explains, as a companion to the evangelist Paul. "I'm sorry. John is away," the woman responds. Disappointed, he explains to the woman that he is writing a history of the movement he has recently joined. This movement was begun by Jesus of Nazareth and was continued with His Apostles and other followers after His death. Luke explains that he left his career as a physician after he heard Paul teach. He wants to know and record everything he can from those who were eyewitnesses to Jesus's life.

He asks the woman, "Are you also a disciple of Jesus?"

"I am."

"Did you know Him? Did you ever meet Him? Did you ever hear Him teach?"

"I did."

"You did? Could I please record what you saw and heard Jesus say?"

"I don't think so," she responds. "You haven't brought enough paper."

"Not enough? How well did you know Him?"

"I knew Him his entire life. I raised Him."

Awestruck, Luke swallows and in a weak voice asks, "You are Mary, the mother of Jesus?"

"I am."

At that moment, tradition states, Luke, the gentile convert, Christianity's first historian, got the greatest interview of all time. Luke never knew Jesus during the Savior's ministry but was likely converted around twenty years after the Lord's Resurrection and Ascension. Beyond his interviews with Mary, Luke collected the recollections of any he met who both saw and heard Jesus teach. Using the Gospel of Mark as a skeleton to frame his history, Luke used these personal accounts to produce what we know as the Gospel of Luke. Later, he wrote a second history, the Acts of the Apostles. Luke's writings occupy more space in our modern New Testament than the writings of any other author.

Imagine Luke's feelings as he wrote the stories Mary told him. He must have scribbled furiously as she recounted the experiences of

THEY
WERE
FAITHFUL.

her cousin Elizabeth and Elizabeth's husband, Zacharias. How they had lived with the agony of not being able to have children for decades. They were faithful. They wanted desperately to be parents, and yet no children came. Then imagine how her face must have lit up as she told Luke about the angel appearing to Zacharias in the temple in Jerusalem. Envision how she must have smiled when she told Luke what Elizabeth had done when the men in their synagogue had wanted to name her baby Zacharias instead of John as the angel had commanded.

Can you imagine how engrossed Luke must have been as Mary described the day when she had been visited by that same angel?

She was an obscure girl in a tiny village miles and miles away from the important leaders and happenings of Jerusalem. The angel had told her she would soon have a child and would name Him Jesus. He would one day be king. Joseph, the young man her parents had arranged for her to marry, had an angel appear to him in a dream, telling him her story was true and that the contracted marriage should move forward as planned. She did not know Joseph well, but his response to this situation was an indication of his character and his relationship with God.

The angel had sent her to live with Elizabeth. God had raised up a friend and mentor for her. Elizabeth understood what it was like to be talked about. Just like the neighbors in Nazareth had likely talked about Mary's unwed pregnancy, Elizabeth's neighbors in Jerusalem likely talked about how Elizabeth was much too old to be pregnant. Yet, when Mary walks into the home of Elizabeth, Elizabeth cries out, "Whence is this to me, that the mother of my Lord should come to me?" (Luke 1:43). Acceptance, kindness, validation. These two understood one another. They loved one another. Mary needed a woman to help her understand pregnancy and delivery, and Elizabeth was there for her each step of the way.

Has the Lord ever raised up a friend for you? Is there anyone in your life you are convinced God placed in your path just when you needed them most? Those are beautiful moments when two people meet and say, "You too? I thought I was the only one." The Lord must smile as He sees you together. I hope you look at your friends that way. I hope you validate and praise them like Elizabeth did Mary. The kindnesses of friends God raises up in our path will be remembered in the eternities.

Mary must have told Luke about the trip to Bethlehem, a village close to Jerusalem. According to Roman law, Joseph had to go to Bethlehem, but not Mary. So why did she go?

She may have explained to Luke how she had been taught the scriptures. She had quoted Hannah's song (see 1 Samuel 2:1–10) to Elizabeth the day she went to live with her. She knew the prophecy of the prophet Micah stating the Messiah would be born in Bethlehem (see Micah 5:2). To go would mean she would

Has the Lord ever raised up a friend for you? . . . I hope you validate and praise them like Elizabeth did Mary. The kindnesses of friends God raises up in our path will be remembered in the eternities.

be giving up the comforts of home; it would mean risking her life in childbirth among people she did not know, yet she knew what she had to do.

UNTO US A SON IS GIVEN

Isaiah 9:6

I can still remember that morning when my own firstborn arrived. I left the hospital feeling like the whole world should pause because of the miracle of what had just happened in the lives of my husband and me. A part of heaven had come to Earth.

When I started teaching my children the Bulgarian language so they could talk with their grandparents and appreciate that part of their heritage, it didn't occur to me that one of the greatest parts of the process would be spiritual in nature—the impact of just three words, often used in farewell and which would become a motto of sorts in our home: Bog e cnac (pronounced Bōg ě snoss).

Translated, it means "God is with us."

This desire to feel a nearness to God, to be close to His peace and power, and to have our lives reflect more of that is something I think we, as His children, all share.

In all our yearnings, though, as much as we try to climb, jump, reach, and stretch ourselves to Heaven, we are still mortal, and in celestial terms, we cannot make it all that far on our own.

I believe God gets this and that is why Christmas is so amazing!

In the Christmas story there is a star and a heavenly host, symbolizing that distant perfection we strive toward. But they are pointing us to a newborn Son given for us—a God who would descend into mortality so that He could understand us completely, so that He could lift us from where we are, so that He could truly be with us!

What a beautiful gift for us as God's children and also as parents and stewards of souls.

In my own family my husband and I have discovered that in our grand visions for our own children, we sometimes try to lead out, expecting them to follow us perfectly and forgetting some of our own struggles to learn and to become. Yet there are times when those children, discouraged by the difficulties of mortality, don't need a line in the sand or a cheerleader from afar. They need us to retrace our own steps and come to them wherever they are so that we may walk with them and so that He may walk with us together.

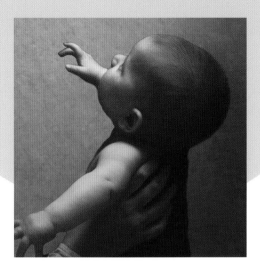

As Luke sat down to write out all Mary had told him, he would pen for the first time a phrase that would be repeated billions of times: "And it came to pass in those days, that there went out a decree from Caesar Augustus, that all the world should be taxed" (Luke 2:1). He then wove together the story she had told him about the inns not having room, the swaddling clothes on which she had likely embroidered symbols of her child's future, the shepherds telling her and Joseph of choirs of angels, and Simeon and Anna in the temple. What was it Simeon had said to Mary? He said a sword would pierce her heart one day. Perhaps to think too long about her son's future filled her with apprehension. Little did she know then the difficulties both she and her Son would face.

Centuries before the Savior's birth, the prophet Isaiah had seen it and said, "Unto us a son is given." Yes, Mary knew one day she would have to share Him with the world. With us. But for a time He was just hers. This story began with the most celestial scene you can find on earth—a young mother caring for her beautiful baby.

THE TENDER SHEPHERD

Luke 2:8–20

Not long ago we attended church in Manhattan while visiting some of our dearest friends. Next to me on the pew sat their wonderful seven-year-old daughter. As the service didn't have a lot to hold a seven-year-old's attention, she industriously used the time to draw pictures and write notes to me.

My first reaction was that of a distracted grown-up absentmindedly commenting, "That's nice," while still trying to pay attention to the speakers at the pulpit. I told myself I needed to stay focused so I could feel Jesus. Then I realized what that amazing little girl was writing.

Jesus is gentle.

I love Jesus.

I love you.

She then traced my hand on a piece of paper. In the middle she wrote, I love that you are, and on the five fingers the words smart, confident, fun, joyful, and messy. I'm especially grateful the last one was a positive in her eyes.

Perhaps Jesus, too, loves that we are messy, with hurts that need healing, shortfalls that need forgiving, seeds of faith still developing, and hearts still being shaped by His profound love.

As I pondered this, I realized there was more of wisdom and love, more of Jesus, on those sheets of paper in childlike scrawl than in most sermons I can recall. Little children seem to have a direct line to heaven. They might not speak the languages of influence or money or authority, but love is their native tongue. Perhaps we can all recall a time when we knew deep down that if we just LOVED enough, we could make, create, or realize our hearts' true desires. A time when we, too, spoke the tongue of angels.

Is it any wonder that the creator of heaven and Earth chose to come here as a baby? Or that the heart of the Good Shepherd is so tightly knit with those of our tender little shepherds?

This piece is about of the wonder and joy with which we approach the divine, a reminder of that we, like little children, can become more like Jesus!

ANTHONY SWEAT

EXCEPT A MAN BE BORN AGAIN

John 3:5

When I was younger, a popular compli-ment was, "Don't ever change!" In light of the gospel and miracle of Jesus's influence, that's a shortsighted saying and a markedly telestial tribute. As Elder Jeffrey R. Holland said about those who come unto Christ and His Church, "Come as you are" but "don't plan to stay as you are."[1] The truth of the matter is that coming unto Christ is a transformative process. The scriptures are full of examples of this divine change: Alma the Younger and the sons of Mosiah, the converted Anti-Nephi-Lehis, early-ministry Peter compared to book of Acts–Peter, Saul to Paul. In scriptural language, this great, transformative change that Jesus offers a person through the divine power of His Atonement is sometimes called "conversion" (see Alma 27:25, Helaman 6:3–4, 3 Nephi 9:20, Luke 22:32, Acts 15:3), or being "born again." "Marvel not that all mankind, yea, men and women, all nations, kindreds, tongues and people, must be born again; yea, born of God, changed from their carnal and fallen state, to a state of righteousness, being redeemed of God, becoming his sons and daughters" (Mosiah 27:25). Nowhere does Jesus teach crucial lessons about this transformative change more clearly than to a ruler of Jews named Nicodemus. And for a Latter-day Saint culture that can sometimes be overly works-centric, checklist-centric, and put-your-shoulder-to-the-wheel-centric, what the Savior teaches Nicodemus is crucial for us.

In this important interview with this member of the ruling Jewish Sanhedrin,

---

1 Jeffrey R. Holland, "Songs Sung and Unsung," *Ensign*, May 2017, 51.

Jesus cuts right to the heart of an issue He discerns that Nicodemus doesn't yet understand: "Verily, verily, I say unto thee, Except a man be born again, he cannot see the kingdom of God" (John 3:3). This saying likely rattled Nicodemus, who as a legalist, checklist Pharisee, perhaps thought that salvation came by his strict adherence to the established rules and observances related to the law of Moses (hand washings, Sabbath rules, etc.)—things Nicodemus did and controlled. But being born again? This was beyond him.

Sensing the profound implications of what Christ has just said to him, Nicodemus asks in return, "How can a man be born when he is old? can he enter the second time into his mother's womb, and be born?" (verse 4). Here we must give Nicodemus some credit. This famous teacher in Israel[2] was not, as we sometimes hear taught in church classes,

actually thinking he had to literally reenter his mother's womb to be born again. He seems to be picking up on Jesus's use of birth as a spiritual metaphor and saying, "How is it possible for me to do that? I can't change myself, especially as old as I am now. I might just as well try to go back into my mother's womb as try to make myself become a new person. This is impossible!" And Jesus's answer was that, yes, it is impossible— on your own. You've got to be born of the Spirit, Nicodemus! The Lord adds, "Except a man be born of water and of the Spirit, he cannot enter into the kingdom of God" (verse 5). We often use this verse to teach about the salvatory necessity of baptism, which is appropriate, but I think there is something more being taught here also: that we need to have our characters divinely changed by the Spirit—something we don't

---

2   Some Bible translations quote Jesus's stinging rebuke about Nicodemus's understanding (John 3:10) as, "'You are Israel's teacher,' said Jesus 'and do you not understand these things?'" (New International Version) or "Are you the teacher of Israel and yet you do not understand these things?" (English Standard Version), implying that Nicodemus may have been one of the preeminent and best teachers in all of Israel at this time.

THIS IS
A GIFT
FROM GOD.

control. This is a gift from God, something that isn't personally earned or checklist accomplished.

Jesus illustrates this to Nicodemus with a metaphor of the wind: "The wind bloweth where it listeth, and thou hearest the sound thereof, but canst not tell whence it cometh, and whither it goeth: so is every one that is born of the Spirit" (verse 8). Nicodemus doesn't cause the wind; he experiences it. Nicodemus didn't control his birth; it happened to him. Similarly, just as you and I don't control the element of the wind and its influence upon us, we don't control the elements of heaven and their spiritual effects upon us. We may (and must) ask,

we may seek, we may desire, and we may strive—of necessity—to place ourselves in the right way to *receive* of its influence, but like the breeze, we aren't in charge of how and when the Spirit comes upon us and causes a mighty transformation in our lives. Go watch a kid try to fly a kite in the dead calm of a summer's day and see how well that works out for him. And go watch someone try to become like God without the wind of the Spirit to lift them up and make them soar. It simply won't happen. You can no more rebirth yourself spiritually than you can birth yourself mortally. It isn't something we do of our own efforts; it is something that is done to us by Christ.

How do we, then, place ourselves where the wind can blow so we can be born again by God? I believe Jesus gives us the answer in this very chapter. He teaches Nicodemus about the love of God. In perhaps the most famous verse in all of Christianity, our Savior says, "For God so loved the world, that he gave his only begotten Son, that whosoever believeth in him should not perish, but have everlasting life" (verse 16). The key to being born again is the divine gift of charity. You can read more deeply about this in the chapter "Encircled in the Arms of His Love." Charity, or experiencing the divine love of God, is the greatest of all the gifts of God (see 1 Nephi 15:36) because it is the greatest in changing us to become more like God. After the resurrected Savior appeared in the Americas, "the people were all converted unto the Lord, upon all the face of the land" (4 Nephi 1:2) and "there was no contention

> The divine love
> of god is the greatest of
> all the gifts of god.

in the land, *because of the love of God* which did dwell in the hearts of the people" (verse 15; emphasis added). Charity converted them, and charity changed them.

I don't think Moroni was describing the *act* of charity in Moroni 7:45. He was describing the *effects* of the love of God upon us—the transforming fruits of what happens to us because of charity. A person who experiences the gift of charity "suffereth long, and is kind, and envieth not, and is not puffed up, seeketh not her own, is not easily provoked, thinketh no evil, and rejoiceth not in iniquity but rejoiceth in the truth, beareth all things, believeth all things, hopeth all things, endureth all things." In other words, a person who experiences charity is born again. President Dieter F. Uchtdorf taught, "This 'mighty change' of heart is exactly what the gospel of Jesus Christ is designed to bring into our lives. How is it done? Through the love of God."[3] General Relief Society President Julie B. Beck taught, "Charity is . . . the

3   Dieter F. Uchtdorf, "The Merciful Obtain Mercy," *Ensign*, May 2012, 75.

Atonement working in us, purifying us, changing us. . . . It's more than benevolence. It is becoming like the Savior, utilizing the Atonement of Jesus Christ."[4] Feeling loved changes people. And feeling divine love divinely changes people.

We learn a lot from the Savior's masterful teachings to Nicodemus. But perhaps the greatest teaching we find is in the simple story of a man who chooses to come to Christ and partake of the love of God to be born again. Whether Nicodemus ultimately

Feeling loved changes people. And feeling divine love divinely changes people.

chose to step into the wind and open his heart to accept that gift is unknown and debated (I like to think he eventually did), but this much we do know: if he did, he was never the same.

---

4   Julie B. Beck, BYU Women's Conference 2011, churchofjesuschrist.org.

INTO THE WILDERNESS

Luke 4:1–14

Shortly after his baptism, Jesus went into the wilderness to be with God. He purposely withdrew from people and the distractions of His community to better learn of and from His Father, spending weeks and weeks of seclusion learning and listening, for what turned into forty days.

Knowing what would shortly come to be, not just for Christ but for all of us, the adversary came wearing many different hats of temptations. He went to Jesus in the wilderness, trying to sell, distract, and alter the Savior's direction with all that is appealing in this life: physical appetites, materialism, popularity, vanity, *power.* Christ hungered, He was physically weakened, and the tempter strategically exploited the appeals of the Savior's human side in the attempt to persuade

Him. From the high place on the temple to the high place of a mountain, the adversary showed Christ visuals from a bird's-eye view of all the wealth, treasure, and bounty of this world and said, *Take.* "All these things will I give thee, if thou wilt fall down and worship me" (Matthew 4:9). In the wilderness, Satan tried to skew truth, to distract, and to get Jesus to doubt who He was and abandon His love, relationship, and calling from God. For forty relentless days, the adversary showed Jesus the lures of men, *everything* a man could want, in desperate attempts to stop Him, to put an end to all that Christ would do (see Luke 4:2–13).

At the end of this experience, Christ taught in the synagogue, where he finally, and publicly, spoke of who He really is. "*I am,*" He announced. "This day is scripture fulfilled. *I am* the fulfilment of the prophesy of Isaiah" (see Luke 4:14–21) Our Savior of the World left His experience in the wilderness ready to begin His work and fulfil his mission on Earth. So why did Jesus not only turn away and leave the wilderness but do so with such a firm resolve to start His work and put into motion all that would unfold?

You.

Saving you. Getting you back. Giving you everything. He is motivated by and dedicated to *you.* His creating this world, His coming here, the miracles, the lessons, the temptations, the struggles, the sacrifices, His death—it was always about and for you. And he never lost sight of that. He never lost sight of *you.*

HE NEVER LOST SIGHT OF YOU.

And with all His love, we are also given a template for how to better recognize the lures of the adversary in our own life and pursuits. When we are becoming a new person, when we are making the time and effort to improve, when we are fulfilling our greater purpose, Satan will absolutely try to lure us away from the Savior and convince us that his own ways are better than the path we are on. The adversary comes to us in our weak times, in our vulnerable times, and exploits them, disfigures them, skews them. He tempted the Savior, "If thou be the Son of God, command this stone that it be made bread" (Luke 4:3), "If thou be the Son of God, cast thyself down from hence" (Luke 4:9). He gets in our mind with similar *ifs* to persuade us to retreat and second-guess, telling us that we should be different or that things should be different. If only things were different, if only you were different, if you were better at *this,* if you were more of *that,* if you had more of . . .

All good things come from God, including thoughts and feelings. Good could not exist without God. Every feeling of happiness, every feeling of comfort, hope, forgiveness,

Every feeling of happiness, every feeling of comfort, hope, forgiveness, strength, laughter, lifted weight, protection, progress, or guidance exists only because God exists.

strength, laughter, lifted weight, protection, progress, or guidance exists only because God exists. All that is good is from and because of God: Every thought we have, even if fleeting, that tells us we can make it through another day, that we can hold out just a little longer and keep going. Moments when we think, *Ah, okay!* Those moments that we can't really explain, moments when our hearts beat just a little bit faster. Goose-bumps moments. Moments when we feel our eyes water and we know if we blink, tears will fall. Moments when we feel our souls jolt and dance within us. Those are the moments when we experience and feel God. They are the moments when God shows us that He is there, that He is participating in our personal lives.

By contrast, anything that is *not* good, thoughts and feelings included, comes from the adversary. If it is not good, it is not of God. If it is not of God, it is not truth; it is not reality. Feelings and thoughts of discouragement— *I'm not worth it. Why bother? I'm the exception. I'm a bad person. I'm not worthy to pray. It's hopeless. I'm helpless. All is lost*—are not good.

Therefore, they are not of God, and are not truth; they are not reality. Even when our lives need correcting, God never does so in such a way as to discourage us but to build us up and motivate us. Correction coming from God comes coupled with reassurance and hope and comfort rather than the contrast of shame or hopelessness. Anything that brings us away from God is the tempter's itinerary, his attempt to lure us away from all that is different than what we have and who we are. Just think of how he got Adam and Eve to hide and retreat in the garden from the only Ones who could help them. He intends to get us to stop, to retreat, to alter direction away from growing into the successful, thriving persons God intended us to become all along.

Isn't it interesting how hard it is for us to see ourselves as God sees us? How unnatural it can be to see in ourselves what God sees in us? How quick we are to see ourselves as less than? How different what we think we deserve is from what He has already strategically and profoundly planned for us? How it is so unconsciously easy for us to sometimes deny ourselves of things because we don't think we are worthy of them or capable of them because surely someone else would be a better fit than us?

But little do we know.

Little do we know what we are capable of doing and becoming because we are *His*.

Regardless of what crooked perspective Satan tempts us to believe, who we truly are is parallel to who Mary was: capable, deserving, crucial, and a profound part of something so much better than we could ever imagine.

And we *are* deserving of God's time and love and dedication. *Why?* Well, because we are His.

He loves us because we are His.

I hope you feel empowered with the knowledge of exactly who you are. Absolutely never forget who you are and *Whose* you are. Your perfect Creator, who crafted galaxies

HE LOVES US BECAUSE WE ARE HIS.

without number, felt the need to create and perfectly craft you. You are needed. Wanted. Essential. Our perfect Creator created you perfectly. How He sees us is the only thing that matters, and He sees each of us as someone capable of becoming like Him. That is the reality. That is power.

It was always about you.

It will always be about saving you. Getting you back. Giving you everything. And He'll never lose sight of that. He'll never lose sight of *you.*

ALONE TO PRAY

Matthew 14:23

I used to be a runner. I say that I "used to" be because today I am more of a TV watcher, a book reader, and an occasional walker, but as a college student at Utah State University, I started running because I couldn't afford a gym membership. When a friend of mine told me I should run a marathon, I thought she was crazy. I had never run more than about seven miles, and a marathon is 26.2. I was not an athlete. I was just a poor college student who wanted a little exercise. But after my friend explained the training and shared her own experience with running marathons, I decided to go for it and signed up for the St. George Marathon. And that's when I began running all over Cache Valley. I ran when it was sunny and hot. I ran in the rain and wind and snow. I ran even when I didn't feel like running. I ran like Forrest Gump.

The people closest to me knew I would sometimes be gone for hours when I went for a run. Once someone told my sister they'd seen me out running past a field at the opposite end of the valley and that I was not going to make it home in time to give her the ride to work she was expecting, to which my sister replied, "Oh, she'll make it." And I always did. But not because I was so motivated and committed. I ran because I was terrified of that marathon looming ahead. And as I ran, I learned a valuable lesson.

Back then, we didn't have the easy access to audiobooks, podcasts, or even music on the go that we have now. Sure, you could listen to a cassette tape on your Walkman, but it was bulky and had wires and batteries and was overall a hassle. This meant that when I went out for a long run, I was essentially alone. And once I got past the discomfort of being alone with my own thoughts, I discovered something powerful available to me. I discovered that for me a long run is the perfect time for deep, meaningful prayer.

Sometimes I prayed prayers of simple gratitude. Sometimes I shared the topics that were on my mind and on my heart and prayed for guidance and strength to navigate them. Many times, I simply noticed the extravagant beauty of the Wellsville Mountains or the Logan Temple set on a hill and marveled at it all. I felt very close to God on my long runs. I felt the Spirit embrace, comfort, and guide. And I believe this was possible because I was

I FELT THE SPIRIT EMBRACE, COMFORT, AND GUIDE.

removed from the distractions of my daily life, making space in my head and heart for me to finally feel those spiritual promptings that had been there all along.

Our Savior understands the power of stillness. He never needed marathon training to motivate Him to remove Himself from distractions from time to time. In Matthew 14:23 we read, "And when he had sent the multitudes away, he went up into a mountain apart to pray: and when the evening was come, he was there alone."

Now that I have four kids, a husband, a cat, and a dog, sending everyone away and heading to the mountaintop to be alone sounds dreamy at times—for me, this would be a running away from something. I believe that for Christ it was a running toward something. He was running toward His Father. Toward stillness. Toward the peace and wisdom available to Him through prayer. And we can do the same.

When the time came for me to run the St. George Marathon, I was nervous. The longest run in my training schedule had been

twenty-one miles, and it was grueling. I had blisters and knee problems from the training, and I was unsure what to expect on that early Saturday in Southern Utah.

In order to beat the St. George heat, the race began before sunrise. I remember waving goodbye to my parents and boarding the bus that took us to the start line. I remember gathering around campfires with other runners to keep warm in the early-morning desert as we waited to begin our journey. There was a buzz of nervousness and excitement. When the race officially began, there were so many people lined up that it took a good fifteen minutes of walking before there was space enough to even begin a slow jog. This was sort of a relief to me.

It provided a nice warm-up and took some of the pressure off. It reminded me that this was literally a marathon, not a sprint.

For the majority of that marathon, I felt really good. I could tell that the training I had done had paid off and the adrenaline of race day had made it even easier. Not too far into the run, as I jogged down a canyon road, the sun began to rise over the red rocks of the Pine Valley Mountains, and once again, I felt the Spirit fill my soul. I felt a peace I cannot describe. I felt an appreciation for the beauty of this earth. I felt in awe of the body I had that would carry me so many miles. I felt gratitude for the people who had organized this event and for the strangers from the small towns we passed through who came out to hand us water and cheer us on. It was a spiritual experience, to say the least. But near the end, everything changed.

I felt my body and my spirit want to give up. My quadriceps were tight from the down-hill slope of the run, and the blisters on my feet were now split open. Several places on my skin were bleeding from the rubbing of my clothes for so long. As I ran down the hill out of Snow Canyon, I could actually see the finish line, but it was still over a mile away, and a mile is a long way when you're ready to give up. I wasn't sure I could make it. I considered just walking, but I knew that would only prolong the pain. My mind raced with options about how to keep moving, and I felt alone. And that's when I remembered that alone time is the best time to hear Him. As I went inward and felt for the Spirit, a stranger from the crowd saw my bib number and the look on my face and called out to me. I will never forget the sound of her voice. "Go 257! You can do it! You're almost there! Don't give up; you're doing an amazing job!"

This life is full of challenges. It's full of pain, both emotional and physical. Sometimes

"You're almost there! Don't give up; you're doing an amazing job!"

that pain is because of a challenge we sign up for, but sometimes it is because of a trial we were simply handed. But within each of us lives the ability to navigate that pain and connect with the source of love and goodness who is God our Father. I worry that in today's world we are not tapping into that source often enough. We are rarely alone with our thoughts and our feelings, unless we make a conscious effort to be so. We must choose to quiet the world from time to time. We don't have to take up running or become experts at meditation, but we must each find the time and place we can be alone to pray, as Christ did. This is our opportunity to connect with Divinity. To receive inspiration and spiritual guidance. To be still.

As I ran the last steps of that marathon, the sun was hot in the sky and I was spent, but just ahead I saw my parents and close friends who had come to cheer me on. Today, many years later, I can still feel their love and enthusiasm as I crossed that finish line. I imagine we will feel something similar when we cross the veil into the next life. Our loved ones will be there to greet us, and we will feel exhausted from the joy and challenge this life has been. At times throughout our lives, we will think it's too hard and wonder if we can make it. But all around us there is support if we choose to be still and ask for it. And we will know as we reach the end of our mortal experience that we have endured it well and that thanks to the Atonement and example of Christ, we are home at last.

IN THE BEGINNING
WAS THE WORD

John 1:1–14

This piece was created from a telescopic image of the Lagoon Nebula, taken at Bear Lake. I love the sheer number of stars and the way they all shine together.

We know Christ as the Creator of worlds, and we know that creation is a significant way in which we can try to emulate Him. Learning to appreciate the majesty and miraculous details of this earth He's given us while using our own creative gifts allows us to shine like these stars, illuminating both the earth and heaven.

JOHN BYTHEWAY

LIVING WATER

John 7:38

Water is found virtually everywhere on Earth in a great number of forms, including oceans, lakes, rivers, streams, glaciers, snow, ice, clouds, dew, and even in the air we breathe as invisible water vapor. Like the air we breathe, just because something is common and abundant does not mean it is not important or vital. Elder David A. Bednar asked an audience of young adults:

What is the most valuable substance or commodity in the world? We might initially think that gold, oil, or diamonds have the greatest worth. But of all the minerals, metals, gems, and solvents found on and in the earth, the most valuable is water. Life springs from water. Life is sustained by water. Water is the medium required to perform the various functions associated with all known forms of life.

Our physical bodies are approximately two-thirds water. Whereas a person can survive for many days or even weeks without food, an individual will usually die in only three or four days without water. Most of the world's great centers of population are situated near sources of fresh water. Simply stated, life could not exist without the availability of and access to adequate supplies of clean water.[1]

Right at this moment, there are robotic probes roaming the planet Mars, sending pictures back to Earth, and testing soil samples. What is it scientists are searching for and hoping to find, perhaps more than anything else? *Water.* Because if there is water, there may be

---

1 David A. Bednar, "A Reservoir of Living Water" (Brigham Young University devotional, February 4, 2007), speeches. byu.edu

life. And there may be a way to support life, especially astronauts, should they someday travel to Mars.

What did water mean to those in Jesus's day?

> The Savior's imagery of "living water" drew upon a long Israelite tradition that water represented important spiritual truths. In the arid climate of the ancient Near East, access to water was crucial for survival, and the scarcity of water made it both a valuable resource and a powerful symbol. The Lord saved Israel in Horeb when Moses miraculously brought forth water out of a rock (see Exodus 17; Numbers 20). The Old Testament prophets Isaiah, Jeremiah, and Ezekiel used water as a symbol of the Lord's Spirit, provident care, and healing power (see Isaiah 41:17–18; 58:11; Jeremiah 2:13; Ezekiel 47:1–12).[2]

Water, by itself, is lifeless; it's nothing but two parts hydrogen and one part oxygen (H2O). What, then, is meant by the phrase *"living* water?" And why did Jesus invite all to come to Him for this living water? The answer can be found in the backdrop of the Feast of Tabernacles celebration described in John 7–8.

The Jews had several feasts or festivals that were held at different times during the year. In Leviticus 23:33–36 the Lord told Moses to hold the Feast of Tabernacles for seven days and a final eighth day of convocation. During the feast, the Jews dwelt in tabernacles, or small booths, constructed in remembrance of the children of Israel who dwelt in tents after Moses led them out of Egypt.

As part of the feast, each day the priests would begin a procession from the temple to the Pool of Siloam, where they would fill pitchers of water, then return to the temple while trumpets played and onlookers chanted verses of scripture, including Isaiah 12:2–3:

> Behold, God is my salvation; I will trust, and not be afraid: for the Lord JEHOVAH is my strength and my song; he also is become my salvation. Therefore with joy shall ye draw water out of the wells of salvation.

---

2 *New Testament Student Manual* [2018], 224.

The Pool of Siloam was considered living water since it flowed freely from the Gihon spring and was not subject to stagnation. Living water was considered most pure and the only water appropriate for ceremonies in the law of Moses.

As the priests returned to the temple, they would pour water from their pitchers onto the altar in supplication for rain and for the success of the crops in the coming year. This procession was such a joyous occasion that it was said, "Who has not seen the rejoicing at the drawing of water has not seen a real rejoicing in his life."[3]

On the convocation on the eighth day, or the great day of the feast, when Jerusalem was full of people who had come for the festivities, Jesus completely upstaged the entire event: After the last pouring of the water, Jesus took the opportunity to declare His identity to the large multitudes. As described by John, "In the last day, that great day of the feast, Jesus stood

LET HIM COME UNTO ME, AND DRINK.

---

3   Tractate Sukkah: Chapter 5, jewishvirtuallibrary.org/trac-tate-sukkah-chapter-5.

and cried, saying, If any man thirst, let him come unto me, and drink. He that believeth on me, as the scripture hath said, *out of his belly* shall flow rivers of living water" (John 7:37–38; emphasis added).

Notice that the water Jesus promised wouldn't come from a well or a spring or a location to which one must travel but would be metaphorically in us. A similar description of having living water within us was given by Jesus to the Samaritan woman at the well:

> If thou knewest the gift of God, and who it is that saith to thee, Give me to drink; thou wouldest have asked of him, and he would have given thee living water. . . . Whosoever drinketh of this water shall thirst again: But whosoever drinketh of the water that I shall give him shall never thirst; but the water that I shall give him shall be *in him* a well of water springing up into everlasting life. (John 4:10, 13–14; emphasis added)

Jesus asks us to follow His example by sharing living water with those around us.

Primary children sing of the little stream who, like Jesus, always loved, always served, and always gave:

> I'm small, I know, but wherever I go
> The fields grow greener still.[4]

When we carry living water within us, we can make things greener, more beautiful, more full of life by sharing what we have with a spiritually thirsty world.

Interestingly, Jesus never said, "I am like gold" or, "I am like precious jewels" or, "I am like riches." The metaphors He used to describe Himself were much simpler and much more valuable: "I am the bread of life" (John 6:35) and "I am the light of the world" (John 8:12)

---

4 "'Give,' Said the Little Stream," *Children's Songbook*, 203.

When we carry living water within us, we can make things greener, more beautiful, more full of life by sharing what we have with a spiritually thirsty world.

and "He that believeth on me . . . out of his belly shall flow rivers of living water" (John 7:38).

Just as water is the most valuable substance for our bodies, the living water Jesus offers is the most valuable element when our spirits thirst, making it possible for us to have our own "well of water springing up into everlasting life" (John 4:14).

THE WATER I SHALL GIVE THEE

John 4:13–14

Creating the image of the woman at the well takes me back to when I was fifteen. I was looking for God in my life, and thankfully, He was looking for me. When I first met the missionaries in Sofia, Bulgaria, it was the beginning of change and serendipity that would set the course of my life in a direction beyond anything I had ever imagined for myself.

After my baptism, the elders told me I would be receiving the gift of the Holy Ghost. I knew so little at the time that I was honestly expecting a wrapped package, and I held out my hands. I soon learned, though, that this was a gift you unwrap with your heart, and when I did, I was filled with a joy and peace unlike anything I had ever experienced. I'm typically a rather happy and enthusiastic person, but now my joy was supercharged. I felt like hugging everyone I came across and telling them just how wonderful and amazing this gift was.

Throughout years of following the gospel path, I've come to find that seeking God isn't a one-time event, nor is the change it inspires in us. Every time we ask, seek, and knock for answers and then follow the inspiration we receive, we allow ourselves to unwrap the gift of revelation through the Holy Ghost and experience that joy anew.

I think this is the message of the Samaritan woman at the well. Here was someone who, in the midst of her daily chores, paused long enough to hear the voice of the Lord. And, hearing Him, she recognized the truth and the significance of what it meant to have her soul's deepest thirst fulfilled.

The idea of a "well of water springing up into everlasting life" (John 4:14) is amazing! It means that every time we ask, thirst and hunger, and drink and partake of God's light in our lives, that light grows deeper and more abundantly within us, expanding our understanding and our capacity to share the wonderful gift we have received.

HOLY, HEALED, AND WHOLE

Luke 4:40

I often say the hardest thing I am asked to go through is the passing of time. When the unwanted and unexpected come my way, I usually welcome them with optimism and faith and excitement to see where they could lead next. Even the toughest of blows I receive during my seasons of struggle have almost always been embraced first with peace in knowing God was intervening.

But then, as time passes and the trial remains, my optimism starts fading and my excitement winds down. My strength starts to thin, and fatigue grows from my efforts. I get to the point where I figure the trial should have ended by then—I've earned it.

Did your eyes roll reading that? Mine did writing it. But it's how I feel. I sometimes feel that if I put in the effort for long enough, I will have earned my blessing of change.

Isn't it wild, all the questions that run through our minds when we feel things should have worked out by a certain time? We might think: *Is God punishing me? Did I do something wrong? Do I have anything left to give? Why would God bring me to this just for it not to work out? How much more am I going to go through? Maybe my faith is in vain. Maybe my efforts aren't good enough. Maybe I'm not good enough. It isn't fair. It wasn't supposed to be this way. Where is He?*

I have spent a great deal of time pleading with God for things to be over or things to be different. I have spent a great deal of time deflated and defeated and doubting as I felt unheard, unanswered, or even unwanted or unworthy. At times it seemed as if darkness would consume me as the sun set.

During one of my many seasons of struggle, I was alone, crawling under the dining room table and picking up things that had fallen when the kids ate dinner. Without any warning to myself, I burst into tears. I collapsed underneath the table and cried an ugly cry for twenty whole minutes. What a sight that must have been.

I was glad no one was around. Not because I was embarrassed or afraid of judgment or anything like that. But I was just too tired and too overwhelmed to try to explain it in words. I didn't even think I could explain it in a way that would really be understood or felt the way I was feeling it. *The sun was setting* and it was getting late into the evening and getting late into this season of struggle. And there I was, alone and out of sight.

As I reflect on this time, I am reminded of the woman who had a blood disease, a season of struggle she had for twelve years of her life. She used every resource and penny she had to find relief and progress and healing, but it just never happened (see Luke 8:43). She must have felt some loss of hope, loss of strength, loss of faith, and perhaps she wondered often whether her life would ever get better. Her life, and

time, kept passing, and it may have seemed to her that the sun was beginning to set on things getting better. And there she was, lost amid the crowd, in the actual dirt, alone and out of sight.

Maybe the woman at the well, too, as she came alone to draw water (see John 4:7), was thinking of the weight of her burdens. Maybe she, too, was thinking about how she wished she could change things and how she wished things were different. Perhaps she went because she wanted to be alone. Or maybe because she felt she deserved to be alone.

These women are not named in the scriptures, but how much we can relate to them! In times when it seems we're out of sight or lost from God, alone, hidden, unnamed, or unimportant, perhaps we are feeling the same things these women felt.

But although they are unnamed in the scriptures, the Savior knows them because He is a *one-by-one* Savior. Every scriptural account of healing and forgiveness occurred one by one as He tended to *diverse* people, to their differences. His love is all-encompassing, individual, and personal.

Our one-by-one Savior is He who stops in the middle of moving masses of people because He notices us on the ground, in the dirt, lost in the crowd. And He comes to us and heals even the hurts we thought were impossible to heal. He purposely travels where others would not, comes to us at our well, and *stays with us*. To help. To connect. To forgive. To teach. To love.

He is aware, He is in charge, and He keeps His promises. He is perfect regardless of passing time because He does not turn His back, neglect, abandon, or play favorites.

He did, and does, come to me when I am alone and collapsed, to pick me up—to lighten, restore, revive, and strengthen—and brings me to something better than what I had in mind.

He sleeps during the storms, not because He doesn't care but because He knows perfectly that all *will* in fact be well regardless of the waves and the wind. He is good even when our situation is not because He is aware, He is in charge, and He keeps His promises. He is perfect regardless of passing time because He does not turn His back, neglect, abandon, or play favorites.

He who exists to bring us to the better, and make us better, travels to us because our one-by-one Savior will never look at us as a waste of time. Our one-by-one Savior is He who is always *yours*.

Even if we are under a table, in the dirt, or at a well—even if it is late into the night, late into our season, late into our life, *even if the sun is setting*—He *does* come. And He stays *and heals*. He comes to us because He doesn't lose sight of us. Because He knows our hiding places. "For [we] are not lost unto the Father" (3 Nephi 17:4). He knows where we are.

And how does He know?

Because we really are His. He comes, with pierced hands on our head, *and heals* us because we are His. That alone makes us enough and deserving. And how much does He love us? Even as much as He hath "graven [us] upon the palms of [His] hands" (1 Nephi 21:16).

Unlike the people in our lives, no matter how resilient and dedicated they are to us, Jesus actually *does* understand. Exactly and perfectly does He know what we're going through, including all our personal differences, and He knows without explanation what we're feeling. He knows all of us because He created all of us.

WE *WILL* FIND PEACE TO OUR SOUL.

What we think is a painful moment alone with a weight we wouldn't know how to explain to anyone else can turn into an intimate one-on-one moment with the Savior if, like the woman at the well, we are willing to listen and be taught.

We may be in a hard season right now, but seasons don't last forever. Just because things haven't worked out yet doesn't mean they won't. We *will* find peace to our soul. Everlasting struggle just isn't in the Savior's cards. Right now, in this life, in this season, while the sun is setting and time progresses onward, we *are* in motion toward greater magnifications—of our blessings, our opportunities, our very lives—that leave us to stand all amazed!

The sun always rises, and you are always the Savior's.

A GIFT OF LIGHT

Matthew 5:14–16

As a visual artist, I am constantly reminded of just how incredible light is. It warms our bodies, hearts, and souls; lights our way; and helps us see more clearly in the dark.

When I was younger, living in Bulgaria and looking for the real source of that light, I was guided to find two missionaries from the Church who answered my question about where that light comes from.

Jesus is the light I was searching for. His light is endless and can never be darkened.

Wow, I thought, I want to have more of that true light.

I've since found that light is a lot like gratitude. The more light we allow to fill our souls, the more desire we have to take that gift and reflect it to others. As we do, the Savior's light flows more through us—what a beautiful thing!

ANTHONY SWEAT

NEVERTHELESS AT THY WORD

Luke 5:1–11

I'm no professional fisherman. In fact, I'm no recreational fisherman. Okay, let me be honest: I hate fishing. But I grew up and live in Utah, I like the outdoors, and I work with young men in the Church, and thus I repeatedly find myself around lakes and fish. So every now and then I dust off a Walmart fishing pole from my garage, grab a few hooks and bait, and try not to look too much like an amateur who doesn't enjoy angling. It usually doesn't take long, however, before I am asking someone else for advice, typically someone a third of my age, questions like: "So how do I tie off this knot so it's stronger?" "What kind of spinner are you using?" And the inevitable, "How do you untangle this line?" It's easy for me to ask and even take direction from a teenager because I simply have no idea what I'm doing.

But talk to me about something I'm an expert on (like driving!) and that's a whole other story. My family knows I have been appointed by an independent and impartial committee comprising of *me*, *myself*, and *I* to be ranked in the top 5 percent of all drivers on the road. Seriously. Come drive with me. Smooth sailing. I'll chauffer the president. If there's a problem on the road, it's not because of me. I was once driving down the highway when my teen said something snarky about my driving and I responded with, "I don't need to take driving advice from someone who can't even tell me which way is east or west," capped off with a smug, "Remember, I've been driving longer than you've been alive."

Oh, how hard it is to take advice when we think we're the expert.

On the shores of the Sea of Galilee, some expert professional fishermen named James, John, and Peter had fished the waters of the lake all night, with no success. Although it's conjecture, it isn't a stretch of the imagination to think they were a bit exasperated and even frustrated. They parked their two fishing boats and began washing out their nets, probably calling it quits. Just then, an itinerant preacher who had traveled at least twenty miles from His landlocked hometown of Nazareth and was a craftsman by trade—no professional fisherman was He!—stepped into one of their fishing boats. Calling to Simon Peter, He asked him to push off from the shore to allow Him to more easily preach to the crowd who had gathered. This likely wasn't the first time Peter had met Jesus, by the way. He had likely encountered the Savior earlier with his brother's testimony and invitation in John 1:40–42, when Andrew told Peter he believed this man was the Messiah. Thus, Simon obliged the boat-preaching request. When the sermon concluded, Jesus said to Simon, "Launch out into the deep, and let down your nets for a draught" (Luke 5:4). I can only imagine what went through Simon's mind. I know what would have gone through mine. *No offense, but have you ever fished this lake? Have you ever even fished?* A teen might as well tell their parent how to drive.

Simon answered him with a justifiable, "Master, we have toiled all the night, and have taken nothing" (Luke 5:5). They had been expertly at this for hours, trying all the tricks of the trade. *And you think a little push-off from the shore and side drop of the net will do it, huh?* Remember, Peter was still getting to know Jesus here. He may have heard or been told that this man was the promised Messiah, but how much did he believe it at this early stage? And while the construction craftsman from Nazareth may be a powerful preacher, what did this man know about fishing in the Sea of Galilee? Despite these rational and justifiable thoughts, Simon did something remarkable, and gave us a lesson, through a single pivotal, humble word: "Nevertheless."

I think the reader of the story should pause between "have toiled all the night, and have

taken nothing" and "nevertheless," letting some silence hang in the air as Peter swallowed any professional pride and submitted to someone he sensed may be the Savior. "Nevertheless at thy word I will let down the net. And when they had this done, they inclosed a great multitude of fishes: and their net brake" (Luke 5:5–6). This miraculous experience humbled Peter to the dust, literally, confirming further that he was in the presence of the divine: "When Simon Peter saw it, he fell down at Jesus' knees, saying, Depart from me; for I am a sinful man, O Lord" (verse 8).

Nevertheless is a powerful word. It is a word that indicates humility, meekness, and a heart that is ready to yield to God. Elder Neal A. Maxwell, who personally learned and spoke often about divine submission, said, "The word *nevertheless* reflects deep, divine determination."[1] Powerfully, our Savior Himself exemplified this same divine determination, uttering submissively in the Garden of Gethsemane, "O my Father, if it be possible, let this cup pass from me: *nevertheless* not as I will, but as thou wilt" (Matthew 26:39; emphasis added). In Doctrine and Covenants 19:18–19, our Savior used the same descriptive word about His atoning experience: "And would that I might not drink the bitter cup, and shrink—*Nevertheless*, glory be to the Father,

---

1 Neal A. Maxwell, "Irony: The Crust on the Bread of Adversity," *Ensign*, May 1989, 64.

and I partook and finished my preparations unto the children of men" (emphasis added).

There's a deep need for us all to learn to divinely submit by saying, *"Nevertheless."* Over and over again the call of the gospel is submission: Be "submissive, meek, humble . . . willing to submit to all things" (Mosiah 3:19); "And now I would that ye should be humble, and be submissive and gentle" (Alma 7:23); "Which sanctification cometh because of their yielding their hearts unto God" (Helaman 3:35). Submission isn't overly difficult when we know we are ignorant, lost, in need, or weak. It is extremely difficult, however, when we are convinced we are right, found, self-sustaining, and strong. Our Savior, His gospel, His Church, and His servants the prophets seem to have little to offer us in such an expert state.

Hard hearts, unrepentant attitudes, critical comments about Church initiatives, Monday-morning quarterbacking of the Lord's servants, and the like can indicate we aren't quite ready or willing to let down our nets. When we trust in the arm of the flesh (see 2 Nephi 4:34),

pridefully rely upon our own wisdom and strength (see Helaman 16:15), and think we are wise and knowing of ourselves (see 2 Nephi 9:28), we can't fully benefit from the strength of the Lord. Paradoxically, weakness in the form of acknowledging an utter dependence on God is what catalyzes divine strength. As Moroni was taught by Christ, "My grace is sufficient for all men that humble themselves before me; for if they humble themselves before me, and have faith in me, then will I make weak things become strong unto them" (Ether 12:27).

Latter-day Saint theologian Adam Miller calls this a "hermeneutics of weakness."[2] Hermeneutics is all about interpretation, and one of Brother Miller's scriptural interpretations is that strength comes only through weakness:

> Weakness names our createdness, our lack of autonomous sovereignty, our persistent dependence on God and his grace for life and agency. In short, weakness names our essential relatedness to God and, thus, our unity with him. . . . To confess our

---

2   Adam S. Miller, *Rube Goldberg Machines: Essays in Mormon Theology* (Sandy, UT: Greg Kofford Books, 2012), 104.

weakness is to confess our connection to him. It follows, then, that if we are humble and acknowledge our insufficiency, his grace will be sufficient. The only thing that could prevent the sufficiency of his grace is our refusal to admit a need for it.[3]

Much like the Apostles during their encounter with the Lord on the shores of the Sea of Galilee, we will never be able to fulfill the potential of our mortal and eternal missions until we are willing to forsake all—especially our own will and expert wisdom—and humbly follow Him as they did (see Luke 5:11). Let us each learn to say that single faith-filled word that indicates a submissive heart ready to yield to God:

Nevertheless.

---

3   Adam S. Miller, *Rube Goldberg Machines*, 104.

THE SOWER

Matthew 13:1–23

"Behold, a sower went forth to sow" (Matthew 13:3), Jesus began while sitting in a boat, addressing "the whole multitude [that] stood on the shoreline" (Matthew 13:2). Around the sloping green hills surrounding the Sea of Galilee, one would likely see workers in their fields, perhaps even sowing seeds at the very moment Jesus spoke. The Savior continued:

And when he sowed, some seeds fell by the way side, and the fowls came and devoured them up: Some fell upon stony places, where they had not much earth: and forthwith they sprung up, because they had no deepness of earth: And when the sun was up, they were scorched; and because they had no root, they withered away. And some fell among thorns; and the thorns sprung up, and choked them:

But other fell into good ground, and brought forth fruit, some an hundredfold, some sixtyfold, some thirtyfold. Who hath ears to hear, let him hear. (Matthew 13:4–9)

This brief parable is rich in meaning. Ancient sowers would cast their seeds in a motion similar to a discus thrower. Interestingly, the word *broadcast* does not come from television or radio—it comes from agriculture: to cast seeds broadly is to broadcast. A family member or servant would typically follow behind the sower and cover or plow the seeds into the ground.

The Soil

Jesus's first parable, however, is not so much about the sower; it is about the different soils in which the seeds may fall. Elder James E.

Talmage suggests Jesus's teaching could be called "the Parable of the Four Kinds of Soil."[1]

The first question to be asked if one wants to plant a successful garden is not about the seeds—it is about the soil. What kind of soil do I have? Preparing the soil for planting is perhaps the most important step since unprepared soil will not produce a harvest, even with seeds of the highest quality.

After Jesus taught, it appears that some listeners walked away unaffected while others stayed and followed with more questions. "And the disciples came, and said unto him, Why speakest thou unto them in parables?" (Matthew 13:10). Jesus answered in part by repeating the call of the prophet Isaiah:

> For this people's heart is waxed gross, and their ears are dull of hearing, and their eyes they have closed; lest at any time they should see with their eyes, and hear with their ears, and should understand with their heart, and should be converted, and I should heal them. (Matthew 13:15)

The words of Isaiah's calling were also a prophecy. Some will have eyes and ears but will not see and hear. Parables both reveal and conceal. Only those who approached Jesus after the initial parable was delivered and asked for more were able to hear the interpretation of the four kinds of soil:

> Hear ye therefore the parable of the sower. When any one heareth the word of the kingdom, and understandeth it not, then cometh the wicked one, and catcheth away that which was sown in his heart. This is he which received seed by the way side. But he that received the seed into stony places, the same is he that heareth the word, and anon with joy receiveth it; Yet hath he not root in himself, but dureth for a while: for when tribulation or persecution ariseth because of the word, by and by he is offended. He also that received seed among the thorns is he that heareth the word; and the care of this world, and the deceitfulness of riches, choke the word, and he becometh unfruitful. But he that received seed into the good ground is he

---

1   James E. Talmage, *Jesus the Christ* (1916), 284.

that heareth the word, and understandeth it; which also beareth fruit, and bringeth forth, some an hundredfold, some sixty, some thirty. (Matthew 13:18–23)

Jesus's further elaboration on the parable mentions oppositions and hazards and, perhaps most valuable, a list of possible weeds that may grow in our heartland: the care of this world and the deceitfulness of riches and, in Mark's Gospel, "the lusts of other things" (Mark 4:19).

Preparing ourselves to receive the gospel deep into our heartland is perhaps the main point of the parable. Once the soil is properly prepared, a seed may be planted. Turning to the Book of Mormon, we find the continuation, the second phase of this parable.

The Seed

A group of Nephite dissenters known as the Zoramites had proud hearts that could be compared to the hardened soil, not willing to accept any new seed. Their prayer atop the Rameumptom indicated that they believed they were elected to be saved, while all others would be thrust down to hell. Perhaps most

Preparing ourselves to receive the gospel deep into our heartland is perhaps the main point of the parable.

63

astonishing to Alma, they proclaimed it had been made known to them that there would be no Christ (see Alma 31:15–18).

However, another group of Zoramites, the poor among them, also approached Alma, and one of them asked, "What shall these my brethren do?" (Alma 32:5). They had been humbled by their circumstances, and because of their poverty and their humility, their heartland was prepared for planting. Alma asked if they would be willing to "give place" (Alma 32:27, 28) that a seed could be planted in their hearts.

The seed he asked them to plant was not a representation of faith, although it would require faith for them to plant it. The seed he asked them to plant was Christ. Alma invited:

> Begin to believe in the Son of God, that he will come to redeem his people, and that he shall suffer and die to atone for their sins; and that he shall rise again from the dead, which shall bring to pass the resurrection, that all men shall stand before him, to be judged at the last and judgment day, according to their works. And now,

my brethren, I desire that ye shall plant *this word* in your hearts, and as it beginneth to swell even so nourish it by your faith. (Alma 33:22–23; emphasis added)

"Plant *this word*" in your hearts, Alma said. Why? And what word? In short, that the Son of God will redeem, atone, resurrect, and judge and that we may "nourish it by [our] faith." Jesus Christ, who was called by John the Beloved "The Word" is the seed for which we must "give place" in our heartland.

The Season
Alma knew, however, that seeds take time to grow. Preparing the soil and planting the seed are only the beginning. Now the seeds must grow roots in order to endure the sun, winds, and weather to come. Jesus mentioned that the seeds that "hath no root" wither away (Alma 32:38). So comes a season—a growing season—of watering, weeding, cultivating, and nurturing. Alma knew that soil and seed alone were not enough to assure a harvest:

> But if ye will nourish the word, yea, nourish the tree as it beginneth to grow, by

PREPARING THE SOIL AND PLANTING THE SEED ARE ONLY THE BEGINNING.

your faith with great diligence, and with patience, looking forward to the fruit thereof, it shall take root. (Alma 32:41)

In order to become a plant, a seed must be nourished with diligence and patience. Having the seed grow strong roots in our heartland is the goal, that it may eventually endure the hazards and we may enjoy the harvest. And what exactly are we growing in Jesus's parable? Grain? Grapes? Figs?

The Supper

After the soil, the seed, and the season come the supper. Alma gives the answer to the question of what harvest we gain from the seed we are planting when he warns of the consequences of not constantly nurturing and maintaining our heartland. What if nothing grows? Alma answers:

> Now, this is not because the seed was not good, neither is it because the fruit thereof would not be desirable; but it is because your ground is barren, and ye will not nourish the tree, therefore ye cannot have the fruit thereof. And thus, if ye will not nourish the word, looking forward with an eye of faith to the fruit thereof, ye can never pluck of the fruit of *the tree of life*. (Alma 32:39–40; emphasis added)

That's what we are growing. Our own tree of life, which is the fourth part of this beautiful parable. The soil, seed, season, and supper all lead to the final result—that we will be able to partake of the fruit of the tree of life, which Nephi called "the love of God" (1 Nephi

11:22) and which Lehi described as "most sweet, above all that I ever before tasted" (1 Nephi 8:11).

To apply the parable to ourselves, we need only begin by asking ourselves, *Which kind of soil am I? When the seed is sown in my heart, is it in a place where it can grow? And are there other seeds in my life crowding out the only true seed? Can I grow roots to help me endure? Now that the seed is planted, how can I let it sink its roots deep into my heart so that I can withstand heat, wind, weather, persecution, and distraction? How is my heartland?*

Lastly, *How can I share the precious seed and harvest with others?* The answer takes us back to the beginning as Jesus taught from a boat on the shores of Galilee: just keep sowing. Share the seeds that grow a tree of life. Cast those seeds broadly; you never know where they may find good ground to grow.

THE TREE OF LIFE

1 Nephi 11:16–23

Trees are among the most beautiful of God's creations. Every tree is a unique work of art that gives us shade, adds variety to the skyline, and marks the passage of time as its branches slowly reach toward the sky. Trees are an eternal symbol. A tree came from a seed, which came from a tree, which came from a seed, which came from a tree, and on and on, forever! Who can find the beginning of a tree?

In one of the most well-known and beloved revelations in scripture, the prophet Lehi declared, "I beheld a tree, whose fruit was desirable to make one happy" (1 Nephi 8:10). What we call "Lehi's dream" is remarkable and unique in that Lehi didn't just dream about others but actually saw himself and his family as actors or characters in the dream. In addition, he witnessed great multitudes, symbolic of the peoples of the world, and watched how they and his family would respond to the tree of life and the other allurements and enticements he saw.

Lehi's dream began in a dark and dreary wilderness, and after following a man in a white robe, Lehi found himself lost in a dark and dreary waste. Why would a man in a white robe, which we assume to be a symbol of help and of goodness, lead Lehi to a place of darkness? Perhaps this angelic figure was not leading Lehi *to* the darkness but *through* the darkness, a symbol of the fallen world through which all of us must pass. After many hours, Lehi prayed. And after he prayed, he beheld. It was as if the Lord turned the lights on, and Lehi beheld a large and spacious field and then the tree, whose fruit was desirable to make one happy.

This was no ordinary tree. This was no ordinary fruit. Not only did it satisfy hunger but it also filled Lehi with joy. Such joy, in fact, that after he partook, he immediately looked for those he loved so he could share the joy. "I began to be desirous that my family should partake of it also" (1 Nephi 8:12).

YOU WANTED OTHERS TO SHARE IN YOUR JOY.

Have you ever tasted something absolutely wonderful or absolutely delicious, perhaps at a restaurant? What did you do? You probably looked up from your plate and said, "Oh, you have got to try this!" In that moment, you were eager to give away something that was yours because you wanted others to taste what you had tasted, and you wanted others to share in your joy!

Lehi looked around and saw Sariah, Nephi, and Sam, but "they stood as if they knew not whither they should go" (1 Nephi 8:14), another profound moment in the dream with an important lesson. Some, wrote Joseph Smith from Liberty Jail, "are only kept from the truth because they know not where to find it" (Doctrine and Covenants 123:12).

Lehi beckoned unto his family with the same words the Savior used, crying with a loud voice, "Come unto me" (1 Nephi 8:15). They came, but Laman and Lemuel were not with them. Of course, Lehi was desirous that his *entire* family would partake, so he called to his eldest sons, but Lehi reports, "they would not come" (1 Nephi 8:18). A painful moment for Lehi, to be sure, since there is a great difference between "*could* not come" and "*would* not come." Nothing prevented them except their own agency.

As Lehi looked around, he noticed other things, such as a river, a rod of iron, and a strait and narrow path. But Lehi wasn't going

anywhere. He uses the phrase "the tree by which I stood" three times in three verses, as if to impress us with the idea of staying put once we have found the light and joy of the tree of life (see 1 Nephi 8:19–21).

Lehi noticed that some commenced on the path and were overcome by a mist of darkness. The thick darkness created a sort of blindness, not only making it difficult for the travelers to see but also isolating them from all others on the path. The effect of such a darkness is loneliness, and as is true in our day, the decision to press forward or give up ultimately became an individual one. Each of us must decide, just as each person in Lehi's dream decided. After much pressing forward,

some arrived at the tree, and Lehi sadly observed that "after they had partaken of the fruit of the tree they did cast their eyes about as if they were ashamed" (1 Nephi 8:25).

This verse describes a pivotal, critical moment—perhaps more important than any other moment in the dream, at least for this group of one-time partakers. Notice that it was *after* they ate of the fruit that they looked around. Were they looking for approval? Were they wondering, *Does anyone know what I'm doing?* It was only after looking around that they became ashamed. The question "What do others think about what I'm doing?" is a powerful influencer for those who are easily influenced. Once Lehi saw that those who were partaking were ashamed, he also looked around to find the cause of their embarrassment, and interestingly, this was the first time Lehi laid eyes on the great and spacious building. He had never even noticed it before.

What do we hope will happen to ourselves and our children when we hear beckoning or ridicule from the great and spacious building? Will we be strong enough to say, "What others say doesn't really matter to me; this is the best thing I have ever tasted," or will our reaction be, "Are they making fun of me? Am I stupid because I like this? Am I not as cool, as sophisticated, or as current in my thinking and attitudes as they are? Should I just give up and join them so I won't risk being embarrassed?" Ultimately, the lease on the great and spacious building will run out, the building will fall, and great will be the fall of it. So what should we do when we hear mocking from the world? Lehi advises and warns, "We heeded them not . . . For as many as heeded them, had fallen away" (1 Nephi 8:33–34).

Father Lehi observed four groups in his dream: First, those who commenced on the path, who were overcome by mists of darkness and were lost (1 Nephi 8:23). Second, those who partook but were ashamed and wandered off (1 Nephi 8:25). Third, those who partook, held fast, and stayed (1 Nephi 8:30). And finally, those with no interest in the right path, who moved directly toward the building (1 Nephi 8:31–32). (Interestingly, these four groups correspond exactly with the four types of soil described in Jesus's parable of the sower in Matthew 13.)

Nephi must have listened intently as his father first described his dream, but he wanted to know more. Much of what we understand about Lehi's dream comes not from Lehi but from his faithful son Nephi. Lehi's dream is contained in 1 Nephi 8. But Nephi's vision of Lehi's dream includes the five chapters of 1 Nephi 11–15. Nephi prayed to know the dream's meaning, and it was as if the angel brought in another screen. Not only did Nephi see what his father saw, but the tree, the rod of iron, the mists of darkness, and the great and spacious building were beautifully interlaced with events in the life and ministry of Jesus Christ. In fact, Lehi never actually calls the

WORDS OF LIFE
BY ADAM TIMOTHY

The word soft falls
On new tilled soul,
Sinks swiftly to the heart,
Where sprouting forth
To sky's expanse,
It seeks the better part.

And, finding rays
Of blessed warmth,
It basks, expands, and grows.
This tasted light
Of truth's delight
Inspires its reaching boughs

'Til gathered clouds
Leave radiance hid,
And thund'rous rolling winds,
Thick billowing adversity,
Press hard on tender limbs,

Which swaying spry
Amidst the squall,
May bend but will not break
As roots hold fast
And deeply drink
Those pools left in its wake.

So tactics change
Withhold the rain
Commence a test much hotter,
Wherein that tree
The depths now plumbs
And finds there living water.

Not stormy hail,
Nor fiery trial,
His love from us might keep,
Fulfilled in all
By faith's pure fruit
Small sown, great grown
To reap.

Then comes anon
One on the path,
Eyes fixed upon the mark,
And presses gladly ever on
Until descends the dark.

The goal once plain,
Obscured from view,
He nothing much does see
But feels the leers,
Hurled taunts and jeers,
At those who seek the tree.

Another sound,
Remembered words,
Form solid in the fist,
Where clinging fast,
The way is felt
To light beyond the mist.

Should darts of fire
Pursue there still,
Quick quenched upon that shield
Of trust in the Redeemer's hand
Love's light to bravely wield

'Til yearning heart,
An hungered soul,
Comes kneeling to partake,
And filled with love,
So sweet alive,
God's word by faith awake.

tree the "tree of life." Nephi was the first to do that in 1 Nephi 11:25.

In answer to Nephi's prayer, the Spirit of the Lord asked Nephi, "Believest thou that thy father saw the tree of which he hath spoken?" Nephi answered "Yea . . . I believe all the words of my father," after which the Spirit cried with a loud voice, saying, "Blessed art thou, Nephi, because thou believest in the Son of the most high God" (1 Nephi 11:4–6). In other words, the Spirit equated the tree of life with Christ! Yes, Christ is the tree!

As in many scriptural parables, metaphors, and dreams, we must be careful not to be too rigid in assigning meanings to symbols. Almost anything good can represent Jesus Christ. The tree that Nephi saw was luminescent as it shone with the Light of Christ:

> I looked and beheld a tree; and it was like unto the tree which my father had seen; and the beauty thereof was far beyond, yea, exceeding of all beauty; and the whiteness thereof did exceed the whiteness of the driven snow (1 Nephi 11:8).

Nephi later testifies that the tree is a representation of the love of God, which reminds us of the words of John, who testified, "For God so loved the world, that he gave his only begotten Son, that whosoever believeth in him should not perish, but have everlasting life" (John 3:16).

Interestingly, the focal point in Lehi's dream is the tree of life, but the focal point of Nephi's vision is the life of Christ. One is the representation, and the other is the reality.

From time to time, each of us may experience tree-of-life moments. Moments when we are overflowing with love, appreciation, and gratitude. Moments when we are surrounded with loved ones. Moments when heaven and Earth seem to connect and we almost literally feel the love of God. In

Each of us may experience . . . moments when heaven and Earth seem to connect and we almost literally feel the love of God.

these moments, we want to share what we have tasted, and we ache for those who may not be with us at the time.

Thankfully, although not specifically described in Lehi's dream, there are many who have left the magnetic pull of the great and spacious building and joined with those who love the Savior at the tree of life and tasted the love of God. This is exactly what happened to Alma the Younger. He was stopped in his tracks by an angel, and he and the sons of Mosiah subsequently repented and left the great and spacious building and made their way to the tree of life. The four sons of Mosiah later left to serve missions among the Lamanites, desirous that others should partake of the fruit. Alma served his own mission among the Nephites and later told his son Helaman:

> Yea, and from that time even until now, I have labored without ceasing, that I might bring souls unto repentance; that I might bring them to taste of the exceeding joy of which I did taste; that they might also be born of God, and be filled with the Holy Ghost. (Alma 36:24)

Like Father Lehi, once Alma and the sons of Mosiah tasted of the fruit of the tree of life, their immediate desire was that others should partake of it also. In our day, the spiritual battle portrayed in Lehi's dream goes on. The great and spacious building will continue to mock and deride, the mists of darkness will intensify, and the strange roads and forbidden paths will increase in traffic. But nothing can compare to the precious fruit that can be obtained without money and without price.

We have also tasted of the fruit of the tree of life. Tens of thousands have served missions, and tens of thousands will yet serve, to lovingly invite more to partake from the tree by which we stand, to taste the light and feel the joy available from this beautiful eternal symbol—a tree of life, a symbol of the love of our Savior Jesus Christ.

TO TRUST HIS HAND

Matthew 6:26

Near our home is a wildlife park where, in winter months, the birds will fly down to eat from your hand. While many of these birds have come to trust the people coming through the park, there are a number that still feel safer if the seeds are thrown about the ground where they can gather them with less risk.

I think sometimes we are like the latter group, wishing God would spread blessings where we can gather them with minimal risk or discomfort. Trying to live the gospel from a safe distance may be possible, but how much we miss out on without that true connection to God!

Partaking directly from the Master's hand requires a spiritual proximity and vulnerability, or an opening of our souls, to trust fully in His love. It requires an all-in kind of commitment.

I remember as a young adult, I struggled with the question of whether to serve a full-time mission. I had only one semester remaining before I would graduate. My visa situation was such that if I were called away from the States, I might not be able to return. Added to that, I was really enjoying my life as it was.

Sometime before, I had received a patriarchal blessing that stated I would go on a mission, to which I thought, Sure I will, one day when I am older, with my husband. Still, the thought of leaving then to serve continued to press on my mind, and I wrestled with it for some time, praying and trying to get my heart in line with God's.

Then one day I felt it was the right thing, and I decided to go. The moment I committed, it was as if this huge weight came off my shoulders. I was about to embark on something difficult, something that might not make perfect logical sense, but I was doing so with my whole heart and putting my trust in the Lord to guide and inspire me to do what He wanted me to do. I learned then that when I trust in His hand, I can partake of His love, His power, and His presence in a way that will never be possible when I am determined to do things my way.

ANTHONY SWEAT

THY FAITH HATH MADE THEE WHOLE

Mark 5:24–34

No local doctors at the time could cure the woman with the hemorrhaging issue of blood.[1] Although the woman "suffered many things of many physicians" (Mark 5:26) and "spent all her living" (Luke 8:43) trying to seek a solution, still the issue "grew worse" (Mark 5:26). Suffering physically, socially, emotionally, and spiritually, where else could she turn?

Then a commotion. A crowd. A chance. The Christ!

On his way to heal the daughter of Jairus, Jesus walked in the midst of a large throng, and the woman "came in the press behind, and touched his garment . . . And straightway the fountain of her blood was dried up; and

she felt in her body that she was healed of that plague" (verses 27 and 29). Jesus, sensing that his radiating healing power had been released, sought out who had touched him. Finding the woman, our Lord said, "Daughter, thy faith hath made thee whole; go in peace" (verse 34).

More attention is given in the gospel accounts to Jesus's healings than to any other single act, including His atoning sacrifice. Of the 3,779 verses in the gospels, 412 (11 percent) are specifically centered on healing stories and teachings.[2] Mark focuses the most on healing, dedicating 19 percent of the verses in his gospel to it. Matthew and Luke both relate twenty-two various stories of healing. It seems everyone was healed, sometimes

---

1   It is uncertain what precisely was the blood "issue" that the woman suffered. Some have called it menorrhagia, or prolonged menstrual bleeding (see, for example Serekara Christian and Baribefe Koate, "The Haematological Perspective of The Biblical Woman with issue of Blood," *Nigerian Biomedical Science Journal*, 14, no. 2 (2017): 25–27.

2   These statistics are by my count. Here are my stats (verses/total verses [percentage]): Matthew 89/1071 (8%), Mark 130/678 (19%), Luke 123/1151 (11%), John 70/879 (8%). Total 412/3779 (11%).

almost on a whim—or in this story, on a thread. We must keep in mind, however, that the events in the gospels—like holidays—were an extraordinary time. A friend of mine from another country first visited the United States on Halloween and saw that everyone who knocked on a door got candy. *What an awesome country,* he thought! He assumed

> Healing was a merciful temporary act used to draw people to Christ.

from what he saw that it happened every day for American children. He didn't understand that Halloween was a once-a-year experience, not an everyday occurrence. It is interesting to me that the whole Book of Mormon records only five accounts of healing.[3] The entire Old Testament has only

fifteen.[4] Of the thousands of believers over the thousands of years, that's not thousands of healings. So why so many divine healings in the gospels?

It was Jesus's healing miracles that initially caused his reputation to spread and people to flock to see Him. Often the gospel writers talk about His "fame" and the multitudes that followed Him in connection to His physical healings and miracles (see Matthew 4:24; 9:26; 9:30–31; Mark 1:27–28; Luke 5:14–15), such as the crowd that followed Him in the story of the woman with the issue of blood. Jesus, however, didn't want to become a sideshow, a traveling performer, as Herod wanted Him to be. "Tell no man" was often the requirement after a physical healing (see Matthew 8:4 or Mark 7:36), such as right after Christ healed Jairus's daughter (see Mark 5:43). Word was

---

3   The Book of Mormon healings are 1. Zeezrom (Alma 15); 2. Nephi raising his brother from the dead (3 Nephi 7); 3. Nephi casting out devils and healing sickness (3 Nephi 7); 4. Jesus healing the multitudes (3 Nephi 17); 5. the disciples of Jesus healing the sick, raising the dead, causing the blind to see and the lame to walk (4 Nephi 1).

4   The Old Testament healings are 1. Sarah (Genesis 18), 2. Abimelech and his family (Genesis 20), Rebekah (Genesis 25), 3. Rachel (Genesis 30), 4. Miriam (Numbers 12), 5. Samson's mother (Judges 13), 6. Hannah (1 Samuel 1), 7. Jeroboam (1 Kings 13), 8. the widow's son (1 Kings 17), 9. the Shunammite woman and her son (2 Kings 4), 11. Naaman (2 Kings 5), 12. the man who touched Elisha's bones (2 Kings 13), 13. Hezekiah (2 Kings 20), 14. Job (Job 42), and 15. Nebuchadnezzar (Daniel 4). I didn't count Moses's leprosy (Exodus 4), as it was a very temporary, albeit grand, lesson to Moses on God's power.

usually always leaked (or shouted!) out, but it's almost like Christ didn't want to advertise physical healing as His main job. So why, then, heal so frequently?

It seems Jesus used his physical healing powers so often in the gospels to provide an external witness to His eternal calling as the Savior. Healing was a merciful temporary act used to draw people to Christ so He could do his long-term soul-saving work with them. For example, He wanted people to know He had been given power to forgive sin. So what did He do? He healed a man of palsy and in essence said, "If I have power to do this (heal), then I have power to do that (forgive sins)" (see Mark 2:9–11). Jesus said the reason for healing the

man born blind was so that "the works of God should be made manifest in him" (John 9:3). "To the intent ye may believe" is what he said of Lazarus's healing (John 11:15). Some of the Savior's most devoted female followers, like Mary Magdalene and Joanna and Susanna, followed and served Him because He healed them of their "infirmities" (see Luke 8:2–3).

Thus, let's remember that fixing physical infirmities isn't what the gospel of Jesus Christ is all about. Christ came to heal us from the sins of the natural man, not the physical pains of the natural world. As one Christian author aptly wrote, "When it comes to miracles, Jesus has a different set of priorities than most of his followers."[5] Because our bodies are mortal, they are going to break down. They will, despite our faith in Christ, eventually debilitate, become diseased, and one day die. After all, the woman with the issue of blood inevitably suffered later hardships. Lazarus died for a second time. The Lord won't heal every physical limitation for every saint, every time, through every priesthood blessing or prayer of faith. To do so would frustrate the purposes of life and God's work and glory. Bodily perfection and healing will come only in the Resurrection, our Savior's "consummate act of healing," as President Russell M. Nelson called it.[6] So what healing does Jesus offer us when we (or a loved one) are sick or hurting or suffering and the source of the pain is *not* taken away?

One word the scriptures often use that gives an answer—including in the story of the woman with the issue of blood—is the word *whole*. To me, wholeness is different from and beyond a physical healing. Wholeness is a unity between body, mind, spirit, and God. Wholeness aligns us with God so that we can accept sincerely, "Thy will be done." Wholeness says, as in the pointed question of Elder David A. Bednar, that we have faith to be healed and we also "have the faith *not* to be healed"[7] (emphasis added). Despite the fact that many of us will experience the miracle of Christ's healing in our lifetimes, inevitably each of us will also have the equally important experience of Jesus withholding that physical healing hand.

In these times, like that of the woman with the issue of blood, although few may see us hidden and suffering in our overlooked crowded corner of the world, let us reach out our heart to the Son of God. Whether we are or aren't physically healed, let us allow the Lord to teach us what He would have us learn and feel from this situation. Let His love and mercy and tenderness come upon us. Let Him align our hearts with God and give us peace. Let Him help make us whole. Even if the malady remains, inner healing can come

5   Philip Yancey, *The Jesus I Never Knew* (Grand Rapids, MI: Zondervan), 1995, 175.

6   Russell M. Nelson, "Jesus Christ—The Master Healer," *Ensign*, November 2005, 87.

7   David A. Bednar, "Accepting the Lord's Will and Timing," *Ensign*, August 2016.

to us through the divine virtues of God's Son, providing miraculous gifts such as increased patience, understanding, strength, faith, acceptance, optimism, empathy, love, and joy. Thus, consistently and profoundly, Christ heals us, even if He does not yet cure us.[8]

Let His love and mercy and tenderness come upon us. Let Him align our hearts with God and give us peace. Let Him help make us whole.

While a miraculous physical healing did occur for the woman with the issue of blood, she was made whole, like the lone leper who returned to give God the glory (see Luke 17:15–19). The greater lesson than healing in the story of the woman with the issue of blood is the truth that the Man who spilled His blood can make us all whole.

---

8   To understand a perspective on the difference between healing and a cure, see Wendy Ulrich, *The Temple Experience: Passage to Healing and Holiness*, (Springville, UT: CFI [2012]), 8–9.

TALITHA CUMI

Mark 5:35–43

Coincidentally, this piece was taken from an image of my own daughter on the day before she turned thirteen. I found this significant because, at age twelve, she was the same age as Jairus's daughter portrayed here. Twelve years also happens to be the length of time the woman with an issue of blood was afflicted, who was healed touching Jesus's robe on His way to Jairus's home. The number twelve appears throughout scripture and signifies, in many cases, completeness and heavenly authority. As such, this image reminds me of Christ's authority to raise us not only from the dead but also from every affliction and difficulty, whether physical, mental, emotional, or spiritual. He makes us whole over the course of our lives.

COME UNTO ME

Matthew 11:28–30

Recently, I read a description of a home for sale. It said:

> Here it is, literally the worst house on the street! The seller has done the hard work of cleaning up the almost half-acre property (it only took 7 dumpsters!), so now is your chance to take it from here. Have you ever watched HGTV and thought, I could do that!? If so, pack up your tape measure and start Googling how to identify a load-bearing wall because it's time to put your money where your mouth is! The roof leaks, the floor creaks, and there's a terrible draft, but this 3-bedroom, 1.5-bath home is very open concept. And by that we mean the inside is open to the outside because several windows are broken. There is a large, sunny window in the kitchen and absolutely nothing else, a wonderful feature for someone interested in a bright reading space (and ordering take out for every meal). And, whether you like to turn up the heat or keep it cool, it won't matter, because there is no HVAC system. Oh, and don't forget about the brick chimney that perfectly epitomizes how we all feel after 2020—about to collapse and going nowhere (literally, there is no fireplace inside the house). What else can be said about this one-of-a-kind opportunity? . . . If you're not interested in crying yourself to sleep every night while you rehab the home, might we suggest tearing it down and building a brand new one in its place? The neighbors would likely thank you.[1]

1 Tracey C. Velt, "Market It," Florida Realtors, blue-soho. mydigitalpublication.com/publication/?i=721090&article_id=4112347&view=articleBrowser&ver=html5.

After sharing this listing with my friends on social media, I read it to my family. As we laughed, I had a thought. What if we had listings for our souls like real-estate agents have for homes? What would my listing sound like? I'm not as good-looking as others. I'm not as brilliant, as rich, or as talented as the people around me. I can no longer run as fast as I used to. My car has so many french fries on the floor they can be counted as my food storage. Sometimes, my family more closely resembles a troupe of professional wrestlers in our pew than what many assume a Church-active family should appear. The other day I got to an event and realized I had left my dress shoes at home. I just wore my suit with my running shoes! I expect it to be a new style any day now. Maybe my listing wouldn't be top-notch.

The previously listed home probably had an owner who didn't treat the house well, but some damage surely occurred to the place that wasn't the owner's fault. Maybe if we were to think of ourselves as a home, we may resemble that real-estate listing more than we would like. Is our foundation stable? Are there rooms we need to clean? Have life's storms battered down our walls? Have there been unkind neighbors or family members who have broken down part of the home? There are things I have chosen such that if my body and soul were a house, it might not be in perfect shape. Some difficulties have happened to my family and me that weren't my choice nor in my control. My family and friends have battled financial problems, betrayal, addiction, lifelong illnesses, and loss. Things have happened due to bad choices, and there are terrible things that have occurred to them through no fault of their own. Life is difficult for everyone. If you look around and think, *Brother Smith, my life*

LIFE IS DIFFICULT FOR EVERYONE.

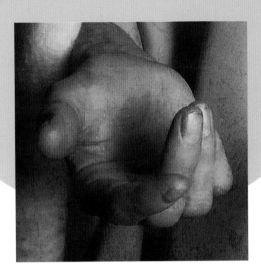

is pretty great. I don't have any serious trials, I say, "Just wait. Difficult times are coming." I don't mean that in a threatening way. Life has a way of spreading out trials to everyone in one way or another. It's not a matter of *if;* it's a matter of *when.*

My life isn't perfect. But I know a Master Builder. In Matthew 11:28, He says, "Come unto me." He beckons but doesn't force. He asks us to turn toward Him. He asks us to repent.

When I was younger, I thought repentance had such a negative sound. It sounded so punitive. It gave me the feeling of getting in trouble and waiting for my Father to either yell at me, give me a firm talking to, or tell me how disappointed He was. It was something to avoid. But the Bible Dictionary defines repentance in the following way: "the Greek word of which this is the translation denotes a change of mind, a fresh view about God, about oneself, and about the world." Did you see that? How does this change your feelings about repentance? How does this change your thoughts about yourself and how God views you? Repentance "comes to mean a turning of the heart and will to God" (Bible Dictionary, "Repentance"), but how often do we think of repentance as a change of mind? Have you ever had a time in your life when

COME UNTO ME

Matthew 11:28–30

This was not an easy series to begin. I had felt a distinct impression to commence work on a project about the Savior, but between dealing with the vicissitudes of motherhood and caring for and then losing my own mother to cancer, a number of years passed without my knowing how or when I would ever start.

Then, around the time the pandemic began, I had another impression. This time I could see in my mind the Savior holding His hands out, beckoning us to approach and receive everything He wants so much to give. With that image in mind, I said a prayer and set to work.

What a relief it was to have made a beginning and to be creating once more. Some hours and many spiritual promptings later, tears ran freely down my cheeks as I lifted my hands to meet those of the Savior's I was depicting through art. I felt myself drawing closer to Christ in a way I had not experienced for some time. In that moment, I can remember thinking, I only hope that someday others might be moved to feel what I am feeling right now, while creating this.

you remember having "a fresh view about God, about oneself, and about the world?" Repentance is a gift, a new starting point. The Lord has clearly stated that we will be forgiven as often as we repent. He doesn't want to shame us; He wants to change us. And He seems ready and willing to give us as many chances as we need to get it right.

Coming to Christ involves turning toward Him. The turn may be large or small. We may be off in the weeds or still on the path. We need to keep moving forward—with a new view of ourselves and the world.

Maybe we feel hopelessly far off the path. Years ago, long before cell phones and GPS, I was on a road trip in the Eastern United States. The longer I drove, the more lost I became. I was trying to visit an old college roommate and was in a state I had never previously visited. I took so many wrong turns that I wasn't even sure I was still in Pennsylvania. The only tool I had was a giant folding map that wasn't very helpful. I had to pull the car over often and asked the locals for directions. Every single person told me something I had never heard before. I would pull up to a store or home and ask how to get to the nearest large city. I kept hearing, "You can't get there from here. You have gone too far. There is no way to get there from where you are."

I was stunned. "What do you mean? Can't I get everywhere from here? Even if I have to backtrack and start over, can't I get there? Can't I keep asking for directions along the way? Can't you draw me a map and give me instructions?"

"You can't get there from here."

It didn't happen once. It happened so many times that I lost count.

Relieved, I finally found my destination. I had been lost for more than eight hours, and during many of those hours, I thought I would never arrive at my destination.

This experience reminds me of my previous idea of repentance. You remember the house from the real-estate listing? Remember, if we consider ourselves as a house, how punishing, dreadful, and arduous repentance seems? Can we take a home like the one listed and repair it? Can we personally repent and become whole? Do we feel like those terrible direction givers and tell the

Savior, "I can't get there from here"? Do we tell Him, "I'm too broken. You can't fix me"?

Would we sit in our broken house when someone offers to repair the roof, replace the foundation, and add appliances? Would we say, "It is too far gone; you can't get the house there from here"? Or would we welcome help? Sister Jean B. Bingham said, "He will not enter without invitation. We must

> He will not enter without invitation. We must come unto Him and allow Him to work His miracles.

come unto Him and allow Him to work His miracles."[2] Invite Him in.

C. S. Lewis said,

Imagine yourself as a living house. God comes in to rebuild that house. At first, perhaps, you can understand what He is doing. He is getting the drains right and stopping the leaks in the roof and so on: you knew that those jobs needed doing and so you are not surprised. But presently He starts knocking the house about in a way that hurts abominably and does not seem to make sense. What on earth is He up to? The explanation is that He is building quite a different house from the one you thought of—throwing out a new wing here, putting on an extra floor there, running up towers, making courtyards. You thought you were going to be made into a decent little cottage: but He is building a palace. He intends to come and live in it Himself.[3]

President Dieter F. Uchtdorf witnessed horrific destruction during World War II. The "Jewel Box" city of Dresden, Germany, was reduced to rubble, including the beautiful Frauenkirche, the Church of Our Lady. For many years, it remained a pile of rocks, but

2 Jean B. Bingham, "That Your Joy Might Be Full," *Ensign*, November 2017, 86.

3 C. S. Lewis, *Mere Christianity* (New York: Touchstone, 1996), 176.

it was eventually rebuilt. President Uchtdorf said he feels the Spirit testify to him that if man can fix a building that has been destroyed, how much more capable is the Lord of restoring His children who have fallen, are broken, or are lost! He said,

> It matters not how completely ruined our lives may seem. It matters not how scarlet our sins, how deep our bitterness, how lonely, abandoned, or broken our hearts may be. Even those who are without hope, who live in despair, who have betrayed trust, surrendered their integrity, or turned away from God can be rebuilt . . . . there is no life so shattered that it cannot be restored.[4]

The Lord invites us, "Come unto me" (Matthew 11:28). It is worth looking at the rest of that verse as well. He says, "Come unto me, all ye that labour and are heavy laden, and I will give you rest." He knows how difficult our lives are. He knows how we feel about

I WILL GIVE YOU REST.

ourselves. If we feel like that house listing, He is telling us that He can help us have peace and we can rest. He is the Master Builder. He has His hands outstretched and invites us to change our view of Him and ourselves.

---

4   Dieter F. Uchtdorf, "He Will Place You on His Shoulders and Carry You Home," *Ensign*, May 2016, 102.

I STAND AT THE DOOR

DOOR

Revelation 3:20

Near our home stands the oldest boarding school in our country. Tucked into the woods behind the school is a cottage where the caretaker of the school resides. This cottage has a beautifully crafted door that I dearly hoped to use in this piece.

One evening at sunset I went up and knocked on the door, interrupting the caretaker and his wife at dinner. As I explained that I hoped to use their door in a biblical piece of art I was making, they were most gracious and accommodating.

Their beautiful door made me think of this scripture. When the Savior knocks, it is very possible that we may need to pause our busy schedules to answer. If we allow our lives to be overly filled with distractions and noise, we may not even hear Him when He knocks. But if we take the time to study, pray, ponder, and reflect, we will prepare ourselves to hear that knock, open our hearts, and receive the Savior's presence in our lives.

BID ME COME UNTO THEE

Matthew 14:25–29

After hearing the news of the passing of his cousin John the Baptist, Jesus departed alone to a desert place to pray. "When the people had heard thereof, they followed him on foot out of the cities" (Matthew 14:13). When He saw the gathered multitude, being moved by compassion, He healed them. Perhaps Christ found healing for His own mourning as He healed others.

His disciples arrived in the evening, suggesting the multitude depart for supper. Christ, not wanting to send the people away, not wanting to depart but wanting a continuance of giving, helping, loving, sustaining, and nourishing, performed the miracle of feeding the 5,000 with loaves and fishes. He wanted to be with them, to give until they were filled.

The disciples then got on a ship to meet Jesus on the other side because He asked them to. And when the winds came, and the waves of the Sea of Galilee rose, he said, "*Come*" (Matthew 14:29; emphasis added). And so Peter stepped out onto the water.

One of the adversary's most successful and destructive strategies in deceiving God's children is to skew our perspectives and our thoughts. The adversary subtly tells us the lie that Christ is sleeping because He does not care, that we are not worth His love. He is quick to point out our failures and focus on our slipups, our sinkings, our shortcomings, our doubts. And in our heads we go over what we are lacking and what we've done wrong and what we could have done differently, and sometimes we wonder, *Why bother?* We doubt ourselves and our faith.

That's what Peter did on the water, and that's what we do to ourselves. The adversary shifts our focus away from the good, from the progress, from Christ, and instead shifts our focus to all that is around us and tells us that *other* things are worthy of our concern, our time. And he gets us to feel bad about our efforts so we will stop making them. He wants us to have an unhealthy and inaccurate perspective so we stop trying, retreat, give up, and *stay on the boat*—so we keep our distance from Christ. His winning game is to get us to wear a negative lens and stay stagnant so that we focus on, and then start believing, that we failed and that our efforts are not good enough, that what we are trying to do is impossible or that the waves are too big, the thunder is too loud, and Christ is too far away.

But before we get trapped in this critiquing, please recognize that *Peter got off the boat.* He tried. He stepped onto the water. He did *something.* And because of his efforts, he experienced and accomplished something new, something different, something *better.*

He did as Christ did; he walked on the water. And he made it closer to Christ because of it.

He who even the winds obey could have stopped the storm at any time, *but He didn't* until *after* He and Peter got back into the boat.

HE DID AS CHRIST DID.

In fact, Peter would never have even been on the boat in the first place if it hadn't been for Christ Himself telling him to.

So what if this account is not even about walking on water? What if it's about coming to Christ *during the storms*? What if He who says, "Come, stay longer, let me fill you," was not sleeping on the boat a year previous because He didn't care but because He knew all would be well regardless of the storm? What if "O thou of little faith, wherefore didst thou

doubt?" (Matthew 14:31) was not a response to Peter's sinking? What if it was in response to Peter's pleading to be saved? What if Christ was saying, "Of course I will save you. How could you doubt that? I am right here. I am out here with you. Did you really think I was going to let the storm hurt you?"

Your efforts, your small steps forward, may seem like slipups and failures, but you are in fact moving forward. You are in fact doing something seemingly impossible. Even the slipups and the smallest of steps are getting you closer to Christ. As Peter knew, safety does not come from reaching for the boat; it comes from reaching for *Christ*.

When I feel the weight of my storms are causing me to sink, I am learning to better grab the helping hand of the Savior—a hand that is always extended, a loving and understanding and an always-there hand, an all-powerful, perfect hand. He has "graven [us] upon the palms of [His] hands" (Isaiah 49:16). Because of course He *will* save.

> As Peter knew,
> safety does not come
> from reaching for the boat;
> it comes from reaching for *Christ*.

LORD, SAVE ME

Matthew 14:25–33

In a storm upon the waters, the safest place is usually in a boat. Yet I love that when Peter saw Jesus some way off, he was willing to set out upon the waves if it meant being nearer to Christ. I think we all find ourselves in similar situations at times, extending our faith and efforts to draw nearer to God and try to live as Christ did, and we too often fall short. Here I wanted to depict the wonder of a Savior who stands solid and steadfast, even upon the roaring waves, and lifts us whenever we call out.

CONSIDER THE LILIES

Luke 12:27–32

While my husband and I were living in Arizona, God told us to move back to New York, where I am from. Having already done a cross-country move *to* Arizona just the year previous, another one so soon was not an easy pack-up for our family of five. But we did it because it was God's idea. We were seamlessly and spiritually brought to a specific house to buy over the internet, we packed up for our eighth time in our, at the time, eight years of marriage, and we sacrificed to complete my seventh cross-country drive. We planned our entire cross-country move around our closing date and thought it best to drive straight through so we could get huge chunks of mileage done while our three very young kids were sleeping. So all five of us, plus our incredibly large dog, traveled 2,300 miles through ten states for the duration of forty-four hours straight with *no hotel*.

And, because of God's guidance, there we all were, on moving day in New York, in front of the house He'd led to us to buy. But after we'd already arrived, we were told we couldn't move in. It was a continually growing list of unexpected and unwanted unraveling that had led to us not having a home to live in. It was out of our hands, so we all crammed into a single hotel room. It was an extremely tight space, the five of us and our giant dog in that single room. During this season of struggle, I could not look at my children without tears streaming down my face. My youngest at the time wasn't even a year old, and I would watch her sleep and be consumed with indescribable anguish wondering how life had led to me not

CONSIDER THE LILIES

Luke 12:27–32

I am a huge lover of wildflowers, so when I learned that the lilies Christ mentioned were these beautiful blossoms of the hills and valleys, it really hit home. If you look closely, you will find a wildflower symbol that I've placed on Jesus's robe in each of these pieces.

To me the phrase "Consider the lilies" is Jesus's way of saying:

"Don't worry. I've got you. I made it all."

"It's in my hands and so are you."

"I have a plan and it's a good one."

"Put your trust in me and I will lead you to a kind of happiness, peace, and glory beyond anything you've ever seen or imagined."

"Do your best to learn, to love, and to grow, but let me be a part of it all."

"Allow me to perform the wonders that only I can so that you might fulfill all you were meant to be as one of God's children."

having a home for my children. How many times would God allow my heart to break from my four-year-old's repetitive question about why we didn't have a home? All of my children's toys, their clothes, our belongings, were packed up and out of sight, all of us having only what could fit in a single suitcase that fit in our car. We had nothing else with us. And weeks passed.

Deep sacrifice is not foreign to me. After I finished college, I was baptized, which came at the cost of my family. It was them or

Could you choose a God you just met over those you've always had? Those you were raised by? Loved by?

God. Could you choose? Could you choose a God you just met over those you've always had? Those you were raised by? Loved by? It took *everything* out of me to move forward in a new way of living, completely alone. And just when I'd thought God could not require *even more* from me, He prompted me to move across the country for my first time, except this time to Utah, and leave behind the only way of living I knew of while trying to cope with the idea that I might never see my dad again.

Taking no thought for my life (see Matthew 6:25) has seemed impossible, illogical, and reckless so many times. But how could I not?

I collapsed onto the floor of the hotel room while we were houseless, yelling at

God with pleadings I have said to Him many times. My body ached from being stretched so thin, from carrying a weight for too long. Aching, then collapsing under the weight I could no longer hold, I told God from the floor, "I'm done. I got nothin' left. I have never felt so thin. My faith, my strength, my optimism—they're just done." I felt like I was left out to dry, and I told Him that. And He responded.

Why won't you let me bless you? Why won't you let me take you somewhere better? That's why I exist!

Do you believe that? He said that to me at a time when we didn't have a home to live in. He said that to me at a time when I didn't have a family to turn to. He said that to me during an entire year of unemployment. He said that to me during a high-risk pregnancy, when the odds were against me. He said that to me every time I have wondered where He was, every time I have collapsed to the ground with my pleadings and the weight I could no longer carry.

God watched His only begotten Son be betrayed, falsely judged, abused, and killed, yet it's said, "It pleased the Lord to bruise him" (Mosiah 14:10). *Why?* Because there was, in fact, something so much more to come. *Something greater.*

As I tally up my losses I am told, "Your heavenly Father knoweth that ye have need of all these things" (3 Nephi 13:32). With humility and desperation I ask myself if I'm allowing God to be God. Am I giving Him the opportunity to show me how great He really is?

"Consider the lilies . . . *how they grow*" (3 Nephi 13:28; emphasis added). They grow! They blossom! They live, they continue, they become something more, something greater. God is good even when our situation is not because He knows something we don't. So what if we got it all backward—all our trials, what we think are missteps or things we want to be over? What if every step is the miracle?

When I allow God to be God, when I allow Him to take me somewhere better, when I see my seasons through, *wow*, does life blossom. Rarely is it what I am wanting or asking for, but it is always truly, profoundly better than I ever could have imagined.

BLESSINGS WILL BLOSSOM.

When it's out of our hands, it's in His. Through the unwanted and unexpected, He is not overlooking or ignoring or punishing but is, in fact, working hard with every little detail to be sure things will be even better than what we had in mind, all of it part of His plan to begin with.

If I am being honest, I wouldn't have a single thing I have now if it weren't for God and *His* ways, including the moments I have yelled at Him, wondering where He was, thinking I couldn't make it any longer. Every single moment has brought me everything I have now—the best things. *My favorite things.* And it breaks my heart to imagine my life any different.

We don't always know the what or the why behind things, but we do always know the *Who*: a God who exists solely to bring us to the better and make us better. Seeing things through one hard or unexpected moment at a time and seeing the blessings that come from that will make it easier for us to trust Him the next time. And the next. And then times will come when we will find ourselves feeling at ease even amid trials, because from consistently trying to trust in Jesus Christ, we will have experienced time and time again that we are being led to the greater things. Times will come when the scary, the hard, and the unexpected turn into exciting, thrilling new adventures that come with peace, with our knowledge that we are in motion to the best-fit blessings. And we'll be profoundly grateful things *didn't* go our own way, because we will find ourselves living as our best self in our best life, experiencing things we didn't even know were available to us, with new knowledge and talents we wouldn't have wanted to go any further in life without. Because we chose to trust the most powerful Being to ever exist.

We will one day pause and look around, and we'll see where we are, what we've gained along the way, the something different and the something greater, and we'll wonder why we didn't do better all along. Because, *my*, how we will have *grown*!

We are promised, "All these things shall be added unto you" (Luke 12:31). *Added.* Losses will be made up. Blessings will be magnified. "The Holy Ghost shall teach you" (Luke 12:12). You will grow. Blessings will blossom. He will take you somewhere better. So "take ye no thought" (Luke 12:11). Embrace the unexpected, knowing who is guiding you. "Fear not, little flock; for it is your Father's good pleasure to give you the kingdom" (Luke 12:32). Every step is the miracle. And you will stand all amazed.

GOD IS IN THE DETAILS

Matthew 17:24–27

My favorite part of this story is how wonderfully creative our Savior is.

When pressed to come up with tax money, Christ probably could have found such a coin in a number of places. After all, if anyone knows how to find that which is lost, including coins, it is Him. Yet He didn't borrow it or find it fallen under a bush or buried under a brick. He asked His disciples, many of whom were fishermen, to seek it in the most unlikely of places and in such a manner as to prove that He had not taken the money from anyone and that He was the Son of God, for only He could have known a coin would be found inside a fish.

Part of mortality is our tendency to forget and become lost at times. Christ's power is in finding and restoring us in the most remarkable of ways. His light, His knowledge, and His love shine brilliantly through the details of our lives. May our eyes be ever open to see them.

CHOOSING THAT GOOD PART

Luke 10:38–42

As a twenty-first-century woman in the world, it is not easy to keep my head straight about what matters. I hope I'm not the only one with this problem. There are so many things I expect of myself that I could never possibly measure up to all of it. For example, I want to be healthy, which means I need to make time to exercise and eat right. I try to cook dinners for my family at least some of the time. I think it's important to keep a clean home, but I also love to style it with the latest trends. Year round there are gifts to be bought and thank-you cards for gifts given to be sent. There are so many tasks associated with raising kids, from teaching them to do chores and keep on top of their grades to disciplining and resetting expectations when necessary. And don't even get me started on the tasks associated with keeping myself looking how I want to look. The amount of time and money that takes is a whole other story for a whole other day.

My point is, while many of these things are part of a modern-day lifestyle and not wrong per se, it's easy to let them get in the way of what truly matters. What truly matters is none of this. Seriously. None of it. The dinners. The grades. It doesn't really matter. What truly matters is something deeper and much more powerful. It doesn't happen on the outside of us. It's not a *doing* thing. It happens inside of us. It's a *being* thing. It is an internal experience of loving

> It is an internal experience of loving others, developing ourselves spiritually, and drawing closer to God in the process.

CHOOSING THAT GOOD PART

Luke 10:38–42

The story of Mary and Martha with the Savior has much to teach us about the power of choice in our lives.

We have within us the power to choose faith, to choose our perspective, to choose to trust God even amid all the craziness of life.

Martha is often seen within the context of one who worries more about the details of the moment rather than the big picture, but I think the Savior's words of encouragement and loving teaching touched her immensely. We certainly see that in the inspired faith she shows in later chapters of the Gospels.

My inspiration for this piece was the idea that, once dinner was done, Martha found the time to "be still" and bask in the light and love of her friend and Savior.

We all have things that seem so big or so difficult in the moment, sources of worry and consternation. Yet this beautiful story shows the power of simply turning to the Lord and hearing Him speak peace and reassurance to our souls.

others, developing ourselves spiritually, and drawing closer to God in the process. That might include some of these activities, but we don't want to sacrifice our relationship with God in the name of any activity. It's the difference between Martha activities and Mary activities. Here's what I mean.

In the New Testament we find a story about two sisters, named Martha and Mary, who are fortunate enough to have the Savior visit them at Martha's home. Martha does what I would likely do if the Savior visited my home. She rushes about trying to be a good hostess. She starts doing things. Nice job, Martha. Very twenty-first century of you. I imagine I would hurry and straighten up my home and

CHOOSE TO TRUST GOD.

wipe down the kitchen countertops, hoping He wouldn't notice the mess. Martha not only believes all this doing is noble but also complains about Mary not helping her. Instead of rushing around *doing* things, Mary sits at the Savior's feet, ready to listen and learn. She is *being* with the Savior, and He reminds Martha of what matters most. "And Jesus answered and said unto her, Martha, Martha, thou art careful and troubled about many things: But one thing is needful: and Mary hath chosen that good part, which shall not be taken away from her" (Luke 10:41–42).

This is a lesson hard learned in today's world. There are so many things to do. Good things. Noble things. And doing those things is not a problem until it interferes with who we're being. There is not a checklist of Martha and Mary activities either. You get to be the judge of when the doing is interfering with the being. But I like to consider the Martha and Mary parts of my life and challenge myself to lean into being as Mary was being.

When I am on a hike with my family, I'm tempted to take and retake photos to capture the moment perfectly. Martha. Alternatively, I could put my phone away and soak up the time with my kids and with nature, knowing that everything I need to remember will stay in my heart. Mary.

When I plan my Relief Society lesson, it's tempting to want to put a lot of time into creating the cutest handout and having a nice centerpiece for the table. Martha. What matters much more than this is the time spent preparing myself spiritually so I can be guided as I prepare and lead the discussion. Mary.

Every night before bed I do a sweep of the kitchen and main living area to tidy up the house before turning in for the night. Martha. But if it gets late and I get too tired, that will take a back seat to the few moments I spend with my husband and children each night before we retire. We choose someone to say the prayer. Everyone says briefly why they love that person, and then the chosen family member offers the prayer on behalf of our family. Mary. Very Mary.

I love the Martha parts of my life. I believe in many cases they are good things. Some of them may even turn into Mary activities at times. But I know that these tasks can easily feel like the most important part of my day when the reality is they are not.

At Christmastime we remember the birth of our Savior in the humblest of circumstances. There were no Martha elements to be found at that scene. There were only Mary situations all around. An exhausted, loving mother. A supportive, kind father. A

At Christmastime we remember the birth of our savior in the humblest of circumstances.

few weary travelers and some unknowing animals. But also a chorus of angels in the sky. A star brighter than is reasonable. And a miracle so complete we can't even comprehend it. An experience of this magnitude is not created by pretty decor or even clean floors. It is only created through the spirit of love, faith, and trust. I truly hope to bring a small semblance of that feeling into my home, into my family, and into my life. I do this through the Mary activities. Let us *be* more than we *do*—as Mary was.

NEITHER DO I CONDEMN THEE

John 8:1–11

This image speaks to my heart of the Savior's profound love and His wonderful combination of strength and compassion. He stooped down to the level of the woman accused, not towering over her in judgment as did her accusers. He remained unmoved by the pressure from and insecurities of those around Him who wanted to stone her. What He spoke to those present, and perhaps what He wrote on the ground, pierced the hearts of those demanding justice and reminds us all of His boundless mercy and power to redeem all who will receive Him.

THE LIGHT OF THE WORLD

John 8:12

During the nighttime celebrations of the Feast of Tabernacles, while four giant candelabras approximately seventy-three feet tall lit the temple grounds and the neighborhoods surrounding Jerusalem, Jesus boldly proclaimed, "*I am the light of the world: he that followeth me shall not walk in darkness, but shall have the light of life*" (John 8:12; emphasis added).

One can only imagine the reaction in the minds of the scribes and Pharisees present on the occasion. What an audacious proclamation! Jesus came not only for Jerusalem, or for Judea, but to be the light of the whole world! Additionally, John the Beloved testified that Jesus "was the true Light, which lighteth every man that cometh into the world" (John 1:9). He lights the world, and He is a light within men and women who dwell in the world.

When we walk into a lighted room, we don't normally bother to look for the source of the light. We don't stop and scan the ceiling in search of the fixture or chandelier. We don't give it much thought, and we often take the light for granted. When the light goes out, however, it becomes urgent that the light be replaced. Not much gets done until we can see what we are doing.

The inhabitants of the new world experienced an episode of darkness with an intensity and duration that perhaps no others ever will: Samuel the Lamanite had prophesied:

Behold, in that day that he shall suffer death the sun shall be darkened and refuse to give his light unto you; and also the moon and the stars; and there shall be no light upon the face of this land, even from the time that he shall suffer death, for the space of three days, to the time that he shall rise again from the dead. (Helaman 14:20)

Imagine the impression a total absence of light made upon the minds and hearts of the people! Not only were the heavens darkened, but

> there was not any light seen, neither fire, nor glimmer, neither the sun, nor the moon, nor the stars, for so great were the mists of darkness which were upon the face of the land. . . . and there was great mourning and howling and weeping among all the people continually; yea, great were the groanings of the people, because of the darkness and the great destruction which had come upon them. (3 Nephi 8:22–23)

When God does an object lesson, the lesson is impossible to miss. During those three days, how could the people cook their food? How could they feed their children? How could they do anything without any light? With all of this in mind, imagine the impact of the words of the Savior when he finally appeared and the very first words out of his mouth were:

> Behold, I am Jesus Christ, whom the prophets testified shall come into the world. And behold, I am the light and the life of the world. (3 Nephi 11:10–11)

Light, so often taken for granted, was withdrawn for a time, and now, after all the destruction and darkness, that light had returned. Would that light be appreciated? Would the Light of the World be acknowledged, honored, and worshiped?

Yes, Jesus is the Light of the World, but amazingly, He shares that name and that commission with us. In the Sermon on the Mount, and in the sermon at the temple in the new world, Jesus declared, "*Ye* are the light of the world" and, "I give unto *you* to be the light of this people" (Matthew 5:14, 3 Nephi 12:14; emphases added).

Those who love light and strive to follow the Savior light the way for others. Sometimes this light is figurative, and at other times, the light is literal. After Moses came down from

Mt. Sinai, "the skin of his face shown; and they were afraid to come nigh him" (Exodus 34:30). While the prophet Abinadi preached to King Noah, Abinadi's "face shown with exceeding luster even as Moses's did while in the mount of Sinai" (Mosiah 13:5). When the missionary brothers Lehi and Nephi were thrown into prison, a cloud of darkness overshadowed the Lamanites, but "through the cloud of darkness [were seen] the faces of Nephi and Lehi; and behold they did shine exceedingly, even as the faces of angels" (Helaman 5:36).

Do these types of stories happen today? They do. Here are just three quick examples: First, President James E. Faust spoke of the beginnings of the Brigham Young University Jerusalem Center and the nonproselyting agreement that students who attend the center must make:

> After the lease had been signed, one of our friends insightfully remarked, "Oh, we know that you are not going to proselyte, but what are you going to do about the light that is in their eyes?" He was referring to our students who were studying in Israel.[1]

Second, a law professor from Japan visiting the United States spent part of his time at BYU. Elder Bruce C. Hafen, while serving as an administrator at the university, reported:

---

1 James E. Faust, "The Light in Their Eyes," *Ensign*, November 2005, 20.

After being on the BYU campus several days, mixing in the dorms with students, he said, "You must tell me about these students and their families. This feels like an island of hope in the time of the apocalypse. What is the secret behind all the shining eyes?"[2]

Third, Sister Gladys Knight, a Grammy Award–winning artist and a convert to the Church, was performing at Disney World when embers of the audience were allowed to submit questions. Someone in the audience inquired, "I have been a fan of yours for many years, yet lately, you have a different light about you. Could you please explain how this happened?" Sister Knight, aware of the diversity of races, national origins, and religions in the audience answered:

> I have learned more about God's standards or commandments that, if obeyed, bring greater peace and happiness. It's not enough to just talk about them, as so many people do. I am now striving more than ever to live them.

> It's not enough to just talk about them, as so many people do. I am now striving more than ever to live them.

After answering some other questions, the director of the event provided a roving microphone for the audience so that others could ask questions directly. Gladys Knight reported:

> A tall, beautiful African American woman near the front said, "Gladys, I am the one who asked about the light you now have. Could you please tell us more specifically how you got that light?"

> Sister Knight was much more direct this time: "I have become a member of The Church of Jesus Christ of Latter-day Saints." She continued, saying, "To the surprise of some of my friends watching the show, the audience suddenly burst into applause."[3]

---

2 *Why I Believe* (Bookcraft, 2002), 159.

3 *Why I Believe*, 187.

THE LIGHT OF THE WORLD

John 8:12

When I first set foot in Manhattan, it was an electrifying experience. There I was, a super-green missionary swimming in a staggering sea of humanity unlike anything I had ever seen. It was this incredible melting pot, where every nationality, race, tongue, religion, ideology, and background one could imagine were gathered on one island.

The diversity was beautiful and inspiring but even more so because of the lens through which I came to see each individual. I learned to look for the light in every person I met. Not everyone wanted to talk or listen, and plenty were hurried or worried or both, but even still there was not a soul that did not carry some semblance of this gift of light. For those who cared enough to take a minute and listen in their homes or as we stood atop a crate in Columbus Square, it was a joy to share what I had come to know as the Source of that light.

These days you don't have to look far to find darkness and uncertainty in the world around you. We even have channels dedicated to 24-hour coverage of exactly that.

When we focus on the light in those around us, in those hopes and dreams common to all mankind, and particularly when we look to the Source of all light, it becomes hard to see much else.

President Brigham Young observed, "Those who have got the forgiveness of their sins have countenances that look bright, and they will shine with the intelligence of heaven."[4]

Jesus is the Light of the World, and yet we are also called the light of the world. How does that work exactly? Jesus Himself told us how we can make His light shine through us:

Therefore, hold up your light that it may shine unto the world. Behold I am the light which ye shall hold up—that which ye have seen me do. . . . And ye see that I have commanded that none of you should go away, but rather have commanded that ye should come unto me, that ye might feel and see; even so shall ye do unto the world. (3 Nephi 18:24–25)

Suddenly, the words of the hymn we sing so often become more than just a metaphor:

There is sunshine in my soul today,
More glorious and bright

"FOR JESUS IS MY LIGHT."

Than glows in any earthly sky,
For Jesus is my light.[5]

Jesus declared at the Feast of Tabernacles that he was the Light of the World. As audacious as it must have sounded then, it was really an understatement. He is the light of so much more. His light is so small that it can start in the eyes of individual disciples and is so large that it can stretch to fill all eternity:

And the light which shineth, which giveth you light, is through him who enlighteneth your eyes, which is the same light that quickeneth your understandings; Which light proceedeth forth from the presence of God to fill the immensity of space—The

4 *Times and Seasons*, July 1, 1845, 956.

5 "There is Sunshine in My Soul Today," *Hymns*, no. 227.

light which is in all things, which giveth life to all things, which is the law by which all things are governed, even the power of God who sitteth upon his throne, who is in the bosom of eternity, who is in the midst of all things. (Doctrine and Covenants 88:11–13)

Jesus Christ is the light that shines around us and within us. We cannot take that light for granted. In a world of increasing darkness, we don't have to be overcome; we don't have to stumble. Our privilege is to walk in the light and to share the light—His light—with the world.

WHAT ARE THEY AMONG SO MANY?

John 6:1–14

This piece represents so much of my work as an artist and as a mother.

God has these glorious plans in mind, yet so often as I begin, I feel like I have so little to bring to the table. Indeed, my work in its infant state is such a far cry from the finished piece that I am often left standing in awe at what God is able to do when I just do my best and let Him work through me.

The thing is, God doesn't seem to mind how much or how little we have to offer. He just asks us for what we have now, today—to lay it at His feet in faith and to trust that His power will magnify our offerings beyond what we could ever imagine.

NOW I SEE

John 9:1–41

Jesus would have made the four- to five-day journey from Galilee to Jerusalem at least three times every year for the solemn feasts: the Feast of the Passover in the spring, the Feast of Pentecost in the early summer, and the Feast of Tabernacles in the fall. Each feast commemorated a different event in history: the Feast of the Passover reminded the Jews of their redemption from Egypt, the Feast of Pentecost celebrated the giving of the Ten Commandments, and the Feast of Tabernacles memorialized the forty-year sojourn in the wilderness before the Jews entered the promised land.

The stories found in chapters 7 through 9 of the Gospel of John took place during the Feast of Tabernacles. During these eight holy days, Jewish families lived in tents outside their homes. It's easy to imagine children enjoying having their parents, siblings, and visiting relatives all stuffed together into tents each night. At this special time, four candlesticks in the temple courtyard, each around seventy feet tall, lit up the night in Jerusalem. For any child afraid of the dark, the Feast of Tabernacles would be a time of safety. The bright light kept the darkness away.

To make the celebration even more memorable was a daily parade-like procession from the temple to the Pool of Siloam and back. The temple priests, accompanied by musicians, wended their way to Siloam and filled a golden pitcher with the pool's living water (water from a natural spring). They then made their way back to the temple and, after a loud blast on a ram's horn, poured the water onto the temple altar.

This was followed by cheers and songs from the congregation. No wonder one Jewish Rabbi once remarked, "Who has not seen the rejoicing at the drawing of water, has not seen a real rejoicing in his life."[1] Tabernacles celebrated God's mercy, His light, and life itself being continually sustained through the water He has given.

It is in this setting that Jesus and His disciples came across a beggar who was born blind. The accepted teaching at the time was that all suffering was connected to sin. It was an attempt to control the uncontrollable. Armed with this teaching, I can assure I never suffer—all I need to do is never sin. This is false, of course, but it must have eased many hearts as they attempted to explain one of humanity's oldest questions: why does suffering exist? For this man to be born blind, someone must have sinned terribly. "Who was it?" the disciples asked Jesus. "Was it this man (a rare biblical reference to a premortal life) or his parents?"

In one statement from the Savior, falsehood shrivels. "Neither hath this man sinned, nor his parents" (John 9:3). In other words, "There is no unfailing connection between suffering and a definite act of sin, my friends." With this statement, Jesus showed He does not fear difficult questions nor the ambiguity created when we don't have the answers.

Jesus continued to explain the wise purpose in the man's blindness, "But that the works of God should be made manifest in him" (John 9:3). In other words, "His suffering doesn't exist because of sin, but because of it, you have a chance to see God's miracles." You have to wonder if the giant candlesticks must have already been lit when Jesus then said, "I am the light of the world" (John 9:5).

"When he had thus spoken, he spat on the ground, and made clay of the spittle, and he anointed the eyes of the blind man with the clay, and said unto him, Go, wash in the pool of Siloam" (John 9:6–7). The same God who said, "Let there be light" (Genesis 1:3), the same God who created man from the "dust of the ground" (Genesis 2:7) could

---

1 "Tractate Sukkah" in *Babylonian Talmud*, https://www.jewishvirtuallibrary.org/tractate-sukkah-chapter-5.

use that same mouth and that same dust to give this man vision. The Light had spoken, and light was on its way.

It may not have happened this way, but I hope it did:

Just as the priests from the temple were wending their way to the Pool of Siloam, this man was also on his way there. As the priests dipped the golden pitcher into the Pool of Siloam, our blind friend dipped his hands in that same water and washed the dirt off his eyes. At the same moment the crowd cheered and sang as the procession returned to the temple, this man sat overwhelmed with joy as his mind began registering what had happened to him. Perhaps he didn't even realize the cheers and the singing weren't for him.

Later this man would face the elite of his society in a heated debate. The leaders of the Jews who had intimidated his parents into silence told him to "give God the praise" (John 9:24) because Jesus was a sinner. Our friend, who up until recently was begging on the streets, did not back down.

THE LIGHT HAD SPOKEN, AND LIGHT WAS ON ITS WAY.

"Whether he be a sinner or no," he says, "I know not" (John 9:25). You have to appreciate his honesty. He didn't believe Jesus to be a sinner, but he was up front about what he didn't know. However, and this is a crucial point, what he didn't know didn't stop him from declaring what he did know. He would not be intimidated by secular authority. "One thing I know," he stated, "whereas I was blind, now I see" (John 9:25).

"What did he to thee?" (John 9:26) they asked. "How did he heal your eyes, then?" The tension was rising! Our friend responded, "I have already told you once, and you refused to listen. Why do you want me to tell you again? Do you also want to become his disciples?" You have to wonder if some were so shocked that they vocally gasped.

Then comes a hurl of insults toward him. He responded in thick sarcasm, "How strange! He healed my eyes, and yet you don't know where he comes from. Aren't you the ones who teach God doesn't listen to sinners? This is the first time in history anyone has ever given sight to someone born blind. Jesus is from God."

The silence that followed must have been palpable. Imagine a red-faced Pharisee responding, "You have been a sinner since the day you were born. Do you think you can teach us anything? Get out."

I would have loved to see this whole scene being described to Jesus. "Then he said . . . and then they said . . . and then he said . . . !" Jesus went and found the man and said, "Do you believe in the Son of God?" The man must have recognized the Lord's voice when he responded, "Who is He, sir? Tell me so that I may believe in Him."

"He is talking to you right now."

Kneeling down, our friend replied, "Lord, I believe" (John 9:38).

You don't have to know everything to have a testimony. You can say, like the man who was healed, "There are some things I don't know, but there are some things I know for sure from my own experience." Be true to the spiritual experiences you've had.

When difficult questions arise, it's okay to say, "I don't know." Don't be afraid of ambiguity. Don't be afraid that not knowing the answer to every possible question makes

When difficult questions arise, it's okay to say, "I don't know."

you look weak. Nobody, including anyone asking you "gotcha" questions, knows everything.

But be bold in declaring what you do know.

C. S. Lewis once said, "I believe in Christianity as I believe that the Sun has risen, not only because I see it but because by it, I see everything else."[2] That has been my experience with Christianity as well. It has also been my experience with the Book of Mormon. I know the Book of Mormon has changed my life, but it has also changed how I see everything and everyone in my life.

When the Lord grants us these experiences, these gifts, we have the courage of Joseph Smith to say, "I knew it, and I knew that God knew it, and I could not deny it" (Joseph Smith—History 1:25).

I know I have had supernal experiences with divinity. I was there. I wrote them down. I can't deny them any more than our friend could deny that he was once blind but then could see. What if the Lord was waiting to see how our friend responded to opposition before he talked with him further? Standing up for the man's first experience with the Lord could have been what initiated more experiences with Him.

You and I will never deny what we've experienced with the Light, because we want more light-filled experiences. You and I will never deny what we've experienced with Him, with the Living Water, because we want to drink again and again.

2   C. S. Lewis, "Is Theology Poetry?", *The Weight of Glory* (London: Geoffrey Bless, 1962), 164–165.

THE GOOD SHEPHERD

John 10:11–15

The books of Matthew, Mark, and Luke are often referred to as the synoptic gospels, because they were written with the "same eye." The first three gospels are similar and can be harmonized, or blended together, easily since they share some of the same stories. The book of John, on the other hand, is unique in a number of interesting ways.

For one thing, the book of John contains no parables, by the strictest definition of the word. Jesus uses several important "I am" metaphors throughout, however, including (emphasis added) "*I am* the light of the world" (John 8:12), "*I am* the bread of life" (John 6:35), "*I am* the true vine" (John 15:1; see also John 15:5), "*I am* the resurrection, and the life" (John 11:25), "*I am* the way, the truth, and the life" (John 14:6), and "*I am* the good shepherd" (John 10:11, 14).

Modern shepherds, more often referred to as "sheepherders," use dogs and pickup trucks rather than rods and staffs. They *herd* or *drive* their flocks from behind, pushing them to where they want them to go. Ancient shepherds, on the other hand, led their sheep and called them each by name. Jesus described Himself as an ancient shepherd, and He is the very best kind:

> I am the good shepherd: the good shepherd giveth his life for the sheep. But he that is an hireling, and not the shepherd, whose own the sheep are not, seeth the wolf coming, and leaveth the sheep, and fleeth: and the wolf catcheth them, and scattereth the sheep. The hireling fleeth, because he is an hireling, and careth not for the sheep. I am the good shepherd, and

know my sheep, and am known of mine. As the Father knoweth me, even so know I the Father: and I lay down my life for the sheep. (John 10:11–15)

The hireling, one who was hired only to watch the sheep, flees at the sight of danger and does not care for the sheep. His motive is self-preservation at the expense of the sheep. The Good Shepherd, on the other hand, faces the danger to the point that He is willing to lay down his own life for the sheep. Why would He do that? Because He knows His sheep and they know Him, and the sheep are His own. Further, if only one little lamb is lost, the Good Shepherd goes in search of it until he finds it, and He comes home rejoicing (see Luke 15:4–6).

Sheep are very simple animals. They are easily distracted, often lose their sense of direction, and at times even need help getting back on their feet when they fall down. "What helpless creatures," we might say, but the prophet Isaiah taught that we are more like those sheep than we may want to admit: "All we like sheep have gone astray; we have turned every one to his own way" (Isaiah 53:6). Going our own way is often the wrong way. Thankfully, the Good Shepherd is willing and able to come after us, at great personal sacrifice, and rescue us from our own poor choices. In fact, Isaiah continues in the same verse, "the Lord hath laid on him [the good shepherd] the iniquity of us all."

And what is His motive for protecting His sheep—us—from danger? He cares for His sheep. Abinadi testified that the Good Shepherd, our Savior, stands between His sheep and the dangers that exist in the world: "being filled with compassion towards the children of men; standing betwixt them and justice" (Mosiah 15:9).

HE WANTS US TO ENJOY AN ABUNDANT LIFE.

Not only is the Good Shepherd concerned with protecting us from danger, but when we are away from danger, He wants us to enjoy an abundant life. "I am come that they might have life, and that they might have it more abundantly" (John 10:10). Old Testament King David spoke in beautiful poetry about the Lord in perhaps the most well-known and most-beloved psalm:

> The Lord is my shepherd; I shall not want. He maketh me to lie down in green pastures: he leadeth me beside the still waters. He restoreth my soul: he leadeth me in the paths of righteousness for his name's sake. Yea, though I walk through the valley of the shadow of death, I will fear no evil: for thou art with me; thy rod and thy staff they comfort me. Thou preparest a table before me in the presence of mine enemies: thou anointest my head with oil; my cup runneth over. Surely goodness and mercy shall follow me all the days of my life: and I will dwell in the house of the Lord for ever. (Psalm 23:1–6)

The Savior has set the example and has shown the way for us to become undershepherds to those around us using the pattern He has set. After the Savior completed his atoning work and returned to Earth as a resurrected being, He visited with his chief apostle, Peter. Three times, the Savior asked Peter if he loved Him (perhaps the Savior

THE GOOD SHEPHERD

John 10:10–15

Roughly thirty years ago, two young men from the States were walking outside a soccer stadium in Sofia, Bulgaria, when they came across a fifteen-year-old girl. I don't believe they would have said a thing to her, but she wanted to practice her English and struck up a conversation with them.

Little could I have known then, as that young girl, how much my life would be changed by the light and message those two missionaries had left their homes to share.

A few years later I got on a plane with a one-way ticket to attend college in America—all my earthly possessions in a single suitcase. Part of me worried what would happen if my luggage got lost, but I realized that even if I lost the little I had, I still had everything because I had God and knew Him. I could trust that the same hand that stretches forth to paint the sunset would also reach out to lift me as I needed.

It's so easy to get caught up in our worries of things both big and small. May we instead find ourselves caught up more and more in those unfailing arms of the Good Shepherd.

was giving Peter an opportunity to soften, in his own memory, his three denials on the night of Jesus's trial). Peter answered each time, "Thou knowest that I love thee" (John 21:15–16), and the Savior's three replies were: "Feed my lambs," "Feed my sheep," and "Feed my sheep." Peter underwent an amazing transformation from sheep to shepherd after the events described in this last chapter of John, continuing throughout his life and ministry.

Today, we remember the words of Peter, who echoed Jesus's words to the shepherds who would come after him in future dispensations:

> Feed the flock of God which is among you, taking the oversight thereof, not by constraint, but willingly; not for filthy lucre, but of a ready mind; Neither as being lords over God's heritage, but being ensamples to the flock. And when the chief Shepherd shall appear, ye shall receive a crown of glory that fadeth not away. (1 Peter 5:2–4)

The Lord's flock has grown. He has many sheep in many folds around the world, and opportunities abound for each of us to take on the role of shepherds and care for one another as the Good Shepherd continues to care for us. President Russell M. Nelson has taught:

> As I foresee the troublesome times that lie ahead—when deepening trials and testing shall be thrust upon members of the Church (see Doctrine and Covenants 1:12–23; 101:4–5)—the gentle caring of compassionate [ministering brothers and sisters] may literally save spiritual lives. . . . The Good Shepherd lovingly cares for all sheep of His fold, and we are His true undershepherds. Our privilege is to bear His love and to add our own love to friends and neighbors—feeding, tending, and nurturing them—as the Savior would have us do. By so doing, we evidence one of the godly characteristics of His restored Church upon the earth.[1]

---

1 "Shepherds, Lambs, and Home Teachers," *Ensign*, August 1994.

"Our privilege is to bear His love and to add our own love to friends and neighbors—feeding, tending, and nurturing them—as the Savior would have us do."

We, too, are often simple creatures. We, like sheep, sometimes go astray. We get lost or distracted, lose our sense of direction, and need help to get back on our feet when we have fallen. In these times, when we are more like a sheep than a shepherd, how grateful we are to be surrounded by faithful undershepherds who look out for us and care for us— ministering brothers and sisters, bishops, Relief Society presidents, class and quorum presidencies—who care about us, and who know us by name. Together, all of us are trying to emulate the Lord, who proclaimed, "I am the good shepherd: the good shepherd giveth his life for the sheep" (John 10:11).

THE ANOINTING

Seest Thou This Woman?
Luke 7:38–50

What would you do if you knew the Savior of the world was coming to your home for dinner? How would you feel knowing he would soon walk through your front door and sit down and eat with you and your family and friends? Any of us would be overwhelmed and ecstatic at the idea. The Lord of the universe is coming to my house for dinner?

This is what happened to a Pharisee named Simon, as told in Luke 7. He invited Jesus, the Galilean teacher, over for a meal. But this was no ordinary teacher. The long-awaited Messiah accepted the invitation and would be sitting across the table from Simon. Simon should have been shocked with joy, and his mind should have been staggered at this phenomenal event, but he was neither awestruck nor staggered because Simon did not know who Jesus was. His lack of spiritual preparation and his self-righteousness left him blind to what was right in front of him. He missed the opportunity of a lifetime!

For Simon, this ordinary meal did become extraordinary, but not because of Jesus. A woman interrupted the eating and approached Jesus. He was lying on his side with his feet outstretched away from the table. She knelt at Jesus's feet and began to wash them with her tears and her hair. She then opened an alabaster box of oil to anoint the Lord's feet. She knew who He was. Here was the awestruck joy. Here was someone who understood what a staggering opportunity this was. She did not speak aloud, but her tears spoke for her, each tear a prayer asking for forgiveness of her sins.

Simon's mind must have been racing. Perhaps he thought, *They say this man is a prophet, but it is obvious he is not. If he were a prophet, he would know how sinful this woman is, and he would never allow her to touch him.*

Suddenly Jesus turned his face away from the woman and toward Simon. "Can I ask you a question, Simon?" he asked. Simon responded, "Yes, Teacher, ask away."

Jesus then told Simon a simple parable. "Two different debtors owed the same man money. One debtor owed him five hundred pence (about a year's worth of average wages) and the other fifty pence (a little over a month's worth of average wages). Neither of them had any money to pay back the debts, so the man forgave them both. Out of the two, which one do you think will love him the most?"

A parable with a simple answer.

"I suppose it would be the debtor who owed more but didn't have to pay it back," Simon responded.

"Exactly," Jesus said. Then He asked Simon a question that can echo within our souls if we will listen. "Do you see this woman, Simon?"

Simon saw a sinner. He saw someone he would never associate with. He saw someone of less value than himself. He didn't *see* her.

Jesus might have been saying, "There is so much more to her, Simon. Can you see it? She is so much more than the labels you have placed on her. She is so much more than the judgments you have made about her. Try to *see* her, Simon."

At this point of the story, we find out Simon hadn't been a gracious host. The simple acts of common courtesy that any guest could expect were not provided for Jesus. Simon hadn't offered water for His feet or a gracious greeting—none of the traditional kindnesses. This was an obvious snub. However, this woman, this sinner in Simon's eyes, provided all of these with incredible humility and compassion.

REPENTANCE AND LOVE FOR GOD FEED EACH OTHER.

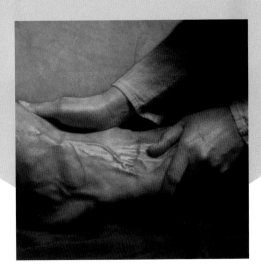

Jesus then spoke to Simon and declared who He was. He said, "Her sins, which are many, are forgiven" (verse 47). Simon would have known only one Being can forgive sins: God. Jesus's claim to forgive sins was a claim to being God.

Then Jesus brought Simon back to the parable by saying, "For she loved much: but to whom little is forgiven, the same loveth little" (verse 47). With this statement, Jesus told Simon who the parable was truly about. It was about the woman and Simon. The difference in the amounts wasn't how much they were sinning but in their willingness to repent. Jesus forgave the woman of the five hundred pence. It was Simon who was forgiven of fifty. In essence Jesus was declaring that those who love Him most repent the most and those who love Him least repent the least. The opposite is also true: those who repent most end up loving Him most and those who repent least don't love Him at all. Repentance and love for God feed each other in a cyclical relationship.

Jesus then turned to the woman and clearly stated for Simon and all in the room to hear, "Thy sins are forgiven. . . . Thy faith hath saved thee; go in peace" (verses 48, 50). With the Lord, repentance and mercy always win the day.

CONTINUE YE IN MY LOVE

John 15:1–11

I am a cliché New Yorker, brimmed with stubbornness and confidence. I have always loved who I was, I never struggled with poor self-esteem, and I've always felt comfortable just being me. I've always been a driven make-it-happen, no-time-for-second-guessing, go-get-it kind of person. And my friends could either come along for the ride, or it was their loss if they didn't, but I was going to keep going regardless.

I was baptized right before my twenty-first birthday, and a few months after that, I followed the Spirit out of New York, all the way to the West Coast. Twenty-one years of confidence, self-love, and stubbornness came in tow with me.

But life and people were different than where I came from. Being completely covered in tattoos with my East Coast flare had set me up for unsolicited stares, rude remarks, parents pulling their kids in closer at the sight of me, assumptions that I hated the gospel and God, and silence from guys my age because *surely* I couldn't have been temple worthy.

I found it difficult to get started in my new chapter of life as well as continue following promptings from God because it was like I was failing before I could even start. How can someone succeed when everything about them in their demographic implies they shouldn't? Anytime I would post my testimony online would even lead to comments and emails saying I should end my life or that *God could never love someone like me.*

I was caught off guard, and I felt unequipped to know how to handle any of this.

And for the first time in my life I was struggling with something very foreign to me: discomfort with myself. And when you are uncomfortable with yourself, you become uncomfortable in too many other aspects because of it—your passions, your promptings, your pursuits. It was a season of loneliness, heartache, idleness, confusion, and anger toward others, myself, and even God.

How do I continue?

At some point my stubbornness started to speak up again. I may have been confused and blinded by who I was and what I was supposed to be doing, but *this* couldn't have been it. I refused to accept that this was just how things were going to be for me. I got tired, ya know? I just got so tired of being upset and feeling down and being mad and being hurt and being still.

Who am I and what is truth? I wondered.

I invested in knowing, because without knowing, I felt as if I was just blowing in the wind. It took a lot of prayer. A lot of pleading with God. Seeking, studying, listening, feeling. A lot of long stares in the mirror. A lot of honest conversations with my Creator. Uncomfortable but life changing.

God really did have only one Begotten Son, and He allowed Him to be mistreated, misunderstood, and killed. *Why?*

Love.

Love for you. Love for me.

And Christ endured, dedicated and committed, through it all—*why?*

Love.

For you. For me.

But how? How could that be for someone *like me*? I look at my differences, and I look at my weaknesses, and I often ask myself *why.*

CHRIST ENDURED . . . FOR YOU. FOR ME.

I mean, who am I? What if I'm the exception? What if I haven't earned His love yet? Or what if I weakened it? When I think of my times of doubts or complaints, and when I fail and fall, I wonder *why* the Lord would ever

want to be yoked with someone like me. But those questions stem from the biggest lie and misconception, that the love of our Heavenly Father and Jesus Christ is inconsistent. *You are not earning Their love, their love is not earned.* It's inaccurately limiting to say that having an unchanging God just means His commandments are unchanging. It also means His love—His love for you and for me—is unchanging, never weakening, and always there.

Why? Well, because we are His.

He loves us because we are His.

When parents hold their baby for the first time, they look down at the baby and are just so overwhelmingly consumed with love. And it isn't because babies have done anything—they couldn't have; they were just born. It's not that babies have accomplished anything to *earn* that love. The parents profoundly and deeply love their child simply because it was theirs.

That is truth.

Our lives have purpose. They have deep meaning. We have godly help and support available at every stage of our lives. And we do not need to be any *more* of anything to feel of our Savior and to be loved by Him.

No matter what you or others think of yourself and your efforts and your setbacks and your shortcomings, Jesus is fighting for you and refuses to leave you and give up.

The laborer in the vineyard asked if he should get rid of the branches that didn't seem to be doing well, but the Lord of the vineyard said, "I will spare it a little longer, for it grieveth me that I should lose the trees of my vineyard" (Jacob 5:51). So there the laborer and the Lord of the vineyard stayed, and the Lord continued to stay there with it.

God is not waiting to love and accept you until you reach some certain standard or qualifying factor. Now is not the time for the Lord to judge us but to continue in His perfect love and revive and forgive and nourish. Now is the time for Him to fight for us and work with us and stay with us as much as He can and give us more chances, more time, more blessings. Because, to the most powerful Being to ever exist, *you matter*. You are worth the effort. He will never look at you like a waste of time. He doesn't want to lose you.

Because of His unchanging love.

And how much does He love us? Even as much as He hath "graven [us] upon the palms of [His] hands" (1 Nephi 21:16).

I'm not sure what part of that seems ordinary or insignificant or what part of it could make us feel anything but empowered. Because if that isn't empowering, then I don't know what is.

To the most powerful Being to ever exist, *you matter*. You are worth the effort. He will never look at you like a waste of time. He doesn't want to lose you.

"This sounds awkward to say, but God loves me, in a sense, almost as much as He loved His Only Begotten Son. At least, I can say this: He gave His Only Begotten Son for me. And that says something about my worth in His eyes. And my worth in the eyes of the Savior. And His willingness to go to Gethsemane and Calvary for me. . . . And what it means to me is that He understands me. That He *loves* me."[1]

I have seen that all that He does is fueled by a never-weakening love and compassion for us. Every time I push myself to trust and see life through, I am shown that He is strategically laboring on my behalf and that everything I am asked to do leads to something *greater*. That's why He exists. That's why all of this exists. It's

1 Jeffrey R. Holland, "The Savior Understands Me" (Gospel Media Library), ChurchofJesusChrist.org; emphasis added.

all fueled by never-weakening love to give us something greater. And we are deserving of it all simply because we are His.

I've given Him too many reasons for Him not to love me. But none of them have changed His mind. When we learn of our perfect Savior, Who made no mistakes, we are also learning of a perfect Savior with perfect *love*. A perfect love is a love that never falters. A love that never fails, never thins, never weakens. A *perfect* love that binds, that lifts, that cures. A perfect love that heals, forgives, carries, renews, and revives.

I don't know the *why* behind a lot of things. But I do know the *Who*. The Savior, who was betrayed, falsely judged, abused, and murdered. In one word, in one single command, He could have put an end to it all. And yet He opened not His mouth. What great lengths He has gone to save us. Jesus died knowing that I might not ever want Him.

What a love. I can live for that kind of love. That absolutely gives me reason and truth to *continue*. "*Continue* ye in my love" (John 15:9; emphasis added).

FEED MY LAMBS

John 21:15–17

I have an eight-year-old son who worries a lot, and this worry causes him to want to double and triple check everything with me.

"So you're going to pick me up from the bus stop after school, right, Mom?"

"Yep."

"Okay."

Then we make dry toast for breakfast because, for some reason, Oliver will only eat his toast dry. In between bites of bread crumbs, the question comes again but worded slightly different. "So you'll be the one picking me up at the bus stop after school?"

"Yes, Oliver."

This continues on, and after about three times of the same question, I lose my patience. "Oliver! Yes! I told you this already. Yes! Yes! Yes! I'm going to pick you up at the bus stop today, just like I do every single day. I've never once forgotten and I'm not going to. You can relax!" I say. And then I feel really bad.

I feel bad because I know what's really going on. I know Oliver already knows the answer to the question he's asking me, which means the reason he is asking is not about learning the answer. There's a different reason behind it—a reason he may not be fully aware of but a reason I can guess. The truth is Oliver is asking this question as a polite way of reminding me not to forget to pick him up. He knows his mom is sometimes a disaster and does in fact forget very important things at times, so the repeated reminders are not a bad idea. Oliver gets nervous easily, and by working to engrain the importance of this task into my head, he is reassuring himself that everything is okay. The truth is there is something tender going on behind this conversation, and therefore the frustrated rant I end up giving is not my best moment.

In the New Testament there is a story that reminds me of this routine Oliver and I go through. Jesus asks Simon Peter if he loves Him. Simon replies that he does, and Christ goes on to ask the same question two more times. Simon Peter gets a little frustrated by the third time, saying, "Lord, thou knowest all things; thou knowest that I love thee" (John 21:17). In reply Christ goes on to tell him each time, "Feed my sheep" (John 21:16–17). As I read this story, I can feel Simon's frustration and imagine the tone of his voice. It's similar to the way I feel when Oliver asks me the same question on repeat. But just as Oliver's question is not really about the question, Christ's question is not either. It's about something bigger. Something deeper. Something tender. Something worth taking a closer look at. I believe this simple but powerful exchange between the Savior and His disciple illustrates two lessons we can take away.

The first comes from Simon's frustrated declaration that the Lord knows all and therefore knows that Simon does indeed love Him. Why would He need to ask a question to which He already knows the answer? I believe it was intended to get Simon Peter's

head into the right place, which gets his heart into the right place. It was a reminder of the importance of navigating his life fueled by his love for his Savior. And we can receive this same blessing by conversing with the Lord through prayer.

When we want to connect with our heavenly parents and feel close to the Lord, we

IT WAS A REMINDER OF THE IMPORTANCE OF NAVIGATING HIS LIFE FUELED BY HIS LOVE FOR HIS SAVIOR.

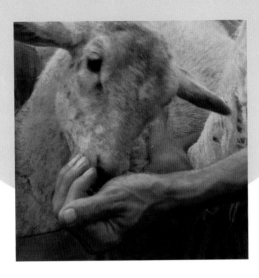

do so through prayer. We open our hearts up either verbally or in our minds as we express gratitude for the things we appreciate and hope for the things we desire. But God is all-knowing. He knows each of us intimately. He knows our hearts and our thoughts and our desires. So why would He need us to tell Him what we're thinking? He doesn't. It's for us. It keeps us operating at our best.

Being a human is hard. Life is unexpected, to say the least. Sometimes the challenges and problems feel never-ending. But if we choose to take our challenges to our Heavenly Father in the name of the Savior, relying on Jesus Christ's Atonement to change us as we navigate it all, we can become refined. As we pray, we focus our minds and thoughts in a way that is powerful and useful to us as we work through our challenges.

We begin our prayers by giving thanks for the blessings in our lives. This gratitude practice has tremendous benefits to us. According to psychologists, gratitude helps us improve relationships, increase self-esteem, and even get better sleep.[1] Perhaps this is why we are taught to pray always. To keep ourselves emotionally, physically, and spiritually healthy through a practice of gratitude.

Next in our prayers, we ask for things we think would be helpful for ourselves or in our

---

1   Amy Morin, "7 Scientifically Proven Benefits of Gratitude," *Psychology Today*, April 3, 2015, https://www.psychologytoday.com/us/blog/what-mentally-strong-people-dont-do/201504/7-scientifically-proven-benefits-gratitude.

lives. This focus on what we want and need (instead of a focus on what we don't want or need, which is much easier for the brain), helps direct our minds toward figuring out how to achieve these righteous desires. With the Lord's help, we can now move forward toward solutions and become better, more Christlike versions of ourselves in the process. And then comes the best part.

When we've gotten our heads and hearts

> We can feed His sheep. We can be ready to serve, to do whatever we can to lighten the burdens of others, and to help bring them unto Christ. And this is when we really begin to feel alive.

into a good place and are achieving progress or resolution around the trials in our lives, we are better equipped to do what the Lord has asked us to do, which is the second lesson we learn from the story in the book of John. We can now stop thinking about ourselves and go help others. We can feed His sheep. We can be ready to serve, to do whatever we can to lighten the burdens of others, and to help bring them unto Christ. And this is when we really begin to feel alive.

As a certified life coach, I get the blessing of watching people move through extremely challenging situations in life to find peace and happiness on the other side of those challenges. Sometimes this journey takes a very long time, and it almost always requires a new way of thinking—about themselves, their loved ones, or the world. It requires the enabling power of Christ's Atonement and results in a truly transformed individual. And once someone gets a handle on a challenge and feels the relief of that progress, they almost always tell me the same thing: "Now that I've figured this out, I really want to help others who are going through this same challenge."

This desire people express is not just a casual interest. I've felt it myself at times, and I bet you have too. It's a pull we feel toward serving others in a specific way, to use our transformative experiences to help alleviate suffering and pain for others. And we describe it as something we know we must do.

It's the kind of knowing that we can't prove but we can't deny either. It's the kind of pull that eats away at us if we don't answer it in some way. And we feel it because within each of us lives the Light of Christ, and when we become refined as we do when we overcome a challenge, that call to feed His sheep wakes up and tugs at our hearts. We get to help bring others unto Christ, just as we were brought nearer to Him through our similar circumstances in the past.

Sometimes I like to imagine that our heavenly parents were like workers in a woodshop when they created us. They paid careful attention to every detail and carved out every part of us to facilitate our development in this life as we worked to become like Them. They created our bodies, our spirits, our minds, our emotions, all with thoughtful attention to detail. And when They went to put on the finishing touches, They wired us to have a desire to help and serve one another. They knew we would need one another's help as we navigated our lives on Earth. They knew that as we learned to love and serve Christ by loving and serving one another, we could access the divine parts of ourselves. What a beautiful plan.

If ye love me, "feed my sheep" (John 21:16–17).

Yes, Lord. Yes.

HE SOUGHT TO SEE JESUS

Luke 19:2–10

While there were crowds in the story of Zacchaeus, here I wanted to portray only the moment of recognition between the chief publican and the Savior. I love that the very wealthy, and likely very proper, Zacchaeus was willing to make a spectacle of himself by climbing above the crowd in order to see Jesus.

I compare that attitude with those in Lehi's dream who became ashamed of the fruit and wandered away from the tree of life because of what others thought or said (see 1 Nephi 8:24–28)—maybe they should have just climbed up into the tree instead. Zacchaeus reminds me that it is only what God thinks that truly matters.

TEACHING IN THE TEMPLE

Luke 21:37–38

One of the most sacred and memorable events of my life thus far was when I was able to sit on the southern steps of Herod's second temple in Jerusalem and teach a group of people. Before we arrived in the Holy Land, a fellow traveler and dear friend said to me, "I just want to walk and be where we know for certain Jesus walked. Will there be sites we know where He was?"

"Yes, for sure," I replied. "The southern steps of the temple mount."

To be on the actual ancient stone steps, only excavated in the 1960s, and teach others where the Savior of the World would have walked to enter his Father's house was a thrill. We gathered as a group, and they sat on the steps while I stood below, sharing messages with them about Jesus's teachings at that very site, and in my mind's eye I could picture Jesus doing the same. "And in the day time he was teaching in the temple . . . And all the people came early in the morning to him in the temple, for to hear him" (Luke 21:37–38).

The temple was central to Jesus's life and ministry. He was taken there to be circumcised when He was eight days old (see Luke 2:21–22). Our earliest account of His youth was Him teaching the doctors of the law when He was twelve (see Luke 2:41–46). When He began His ministry, He was tempted on the pinnacle of the temple (see Matthew 4:5). He cleansed the temple of money changers, seemingly for the first time, in John 2:13–17. At the temple our Lord gave a sermon on the divine law of witnesses (see John 5) and another sermon on His doctrine at the Feast of Tabernacles, confounding His critics with His answers (see John 7). The story of the woman taken in adultery in John 8 and the Lord's profound teachings about self-righteous judgment and unnecessary condemnation took place in the temple. In Mark 11:15 the Lord cleansed the temple again. His discourse on His divine authority took place at the temple (see Mark 11:27–33), as did His teachings on the two great commandments (see Mark 12:28–31) and the widow's mite (see Mark 12:41–44).

It reasons, then, that the holy temple would be central to the Lord's restored Church in the latter days also. While there are many reasons I believe in the Restoration, the emphasis on the temple as the center of all our worship, with its ordinances and covenants, is key. President Russell M. Nelson taught, "The temple is the object of every activity, every lesson, every progressive step in the Church. All of our efforts in [the Church] lead to the holy temple."[1] What other faith on the earth is talking about temples, the priesthood offering of modern sons and daughters of Levi for the salvation of the dead (see Doctrine and Covenants 128:24), the covenants of Abra-ham, sealings of couples and families, and endowments

of knowledge and power? As early as 1832 the Lord was focusing the newly formed restored Church on the centrality of the temple, teaching about the New Jerusalem and a temple at its center in a pattern after the

> "Build a house unto me . . . Yea, and my presence shall be there, for I will come into it, and all the pure in heart that shall come into it shall see God."

temple in ancient Jerusalem (see Doctrine and Covenants 84:2–4).

Concerning this latter-day temple, we learn that "a cloud shall rest upon it, which cloud shall be even the glory of the Lord, which shall fill the house" (verse 5). The Lord promised His presence in His temples of the Latter-days: "Build a house unto me . . . Yea, and my presence shall be there, for I will come into it, and all the pure in heart that shall come into it shall see God" (Doctrine and

---

1   Russell M. Nelson, "Prepare for the Blessings of the Temple," *Ensign*, October 2010, 41.

Covenants 97:15–16). When Joseph Smith dedicated the Kirtland Temple, he prayed that the Lord's "holy presence may be continually in this house" (Doctrine and Covenants 109:12). The Lord honored that prayer shortly thereafter with His literal presence (see Doctrine and Covenants 110:1–10), promising Joseph Smith and Oliver Cowdery, "My name shall be here; and I will manifest myself to my people in mercy in this house. Yea, I will appear unto my servants, and speak unto them with mine own voice" (Doctrine and Covenants 110:7–8).

I was once in the celestial room of the Salt Lake Temple with a group, and we were conversing about President Lorenzo Snow's vision of the Savior in the temple. One of our group said, "I think we're standing right about where it is reported He appeared." As we talked, an old temple worker shuffled over to us. I thought he was going to tell us to keep our voices down. Instead, he said something like, "Do you realize you guys are standing right where it is reported that the Savior appeared to Lorenzo Snow?" We began to excitedly talk with him about it. Just then I saw another temple worker look at us from across the room and make her way over. She opened her mouth to talk. I was ready for a mild reminder to be quieter. Instead, she said, "Do you know you're standing right where the Lord appeared to Lorenzo Snow?"

While I believe the Lord has literally manifested Himself to His servants and people in

FOR TO HEAR HIM

Luke 21:37–38

In Luke 21:38 word spreads that Jesus is going to be at the temple teaching the next day: "And all the people came early in the morning to him in the temple, for to hear him."

All the people must have been some crowd, setting off before the crack of dawn to find a good spot so they could be close enough to hear for themselves Jesus teaching.

Reading that made me want to be a better hearer, someone who listens with real intent to the things I need most.

Listening in this manner means opening ourselves to the Spirit's whispering and ideas and dreams and visions of what we are meant to say and do and be.

There is an absolute cacophony of voices within us and around us. Many of them are urgent and loud, ranging from doubt and distrust to entertaining to shocking. Too often we lend our ears and our attention to this demanding yet empty noise.

We can learn to tune our hearing instead to the voices that pierce quietly through the noise and reach our souls.

Once we've learned that, we are ready to turn our hearts and ears to our children, hearing more intently what they feel and are working to become. Some of that is unspoken but can be heard if we are still enough. Some of it is tentatively voiced and reaches us only once we are fully focused, present, all ears. When we do this, I believe something remarkable transpires. The simple gift of listening becomes the power to launch ourselves and others beyond the gravity of self-doubt, envy, and ennui, teaching the hearer to listen bravely to that voice within themselves. And, hearing it, to follow.

the temple, it is important to acknowledge that God manifests Himself in many ways to His children, as His wisdom, will, and timing dictate (see Doctrine and Covenants 88:68). As President Henry B. Eyring taught:

> President Russell M. Nelson made clear for us that we can "see" the Savior in the temple in the sense that He becomes no longer unknown to us. President Nelson said this: "We understand Him. We comprehend His work and His glory. And we begin to feel the infinite impact of His matchless life." If you or I should go to the temple insufficiently pure, we would not be able to see, by the power of the Holy Ghost, the spiritual teaching about the Savior that we can receive in the temple. When we are worthy to receive such teaching, there can grow through our temple experience hope, joy, and optimism throughout our lives.[2]

While the teachings in the holy temple certainly center on the Savior, the temple is unique in that it is where you go to not only be taught *about* the Lord but *by* the Lord. The temple is His house of learning. Years ago, while I drove by yet another temple in Utah, one of my young children said to me, "Jesus sure has a lot of houses." And I said, "That's because He sure has a lot of people to teach." And I really believe that.

Just like we often find Jesus teaching at the temple in the New Testament, the temple remains the central place for Him to be found teaching today. Those who visit the Lord's holy house and worship often therein will find Him "teaching in the temple" (Luke 21:37), just as He's always done.

THE TEMPLE IS HIS HOUSE OF LEARNING.

---

2   Henry B. Eyring, "I Love to See the Temple," *Liahona*, May 2021, 30.

THE BREAD OF LIFE

Luke 22:19

As the hills of Galilee were beginning to be covered in green grass each spring, the Savior and his disciples, along with hundreds of other families, made the four- to five-day journey to Jerusalem for Passover. This holy day was set apart to commemorate the angel of death passing over the homes of the Israelites when they were slaves in Egypt. Faithful Jews dedicated this time to remembering what the Lord had done for their ancestors.

The Passover meal, with its unleavened bread (a reminder of the pressure of exiting Egypt), salt water (representing the tears of the enslaved), and the bitter herbs (a reminder of the pain of bondage and slavery), revolved around a sacrificial lamb, which could only be sacrificed at the temple in Jerusalem. The lamb had to "be without blemish, a male of the first year . . ." (Exodus 12:5), and the people were commanded, "neither shall ye break a bone thereof" (Exodus 12:46). The lamb's blood was daubed on the entrance to the home on each side (doorposts) and the lintel (the beam across the top) during the final plague of Egypt. The blood was a sign of obedience, which protected the ancient Israelites from the angel of death.

This paschal (Passover) lamb would then be roasted, and the family would consume all of it with the unleavened bread, bitter herbs, and wine. The patriarch of the family would tell the story of Moses and Pharaoh, the plagues, and the escape of the Israelites through the Red Sea. As the family members prepared and focused, they put themselves in the story. As they participated in the Passover meal, they were coming out of Egypt and were delivered by the Lord. They saw the tears of their ancestors, they felt their pain, and they rejoiced in God's deliverance. Anything left of the lamb (the bones and other inedible parts) were to be burned with fire. They ate the meal quickly with their shoes on and walking sticks in their hands, representing the fast departure from Egypt.

The Gospel of John records three events crucial to connecting Jesus to the Passover: the declaration of John the Baptist, the Savior turning water into wine, and the Bread of Life sermon. Each of these events enables us to connect more to the Lord's sacrifice on our behalf and its weekly commemoration through the partaking of the sacrament. These stories can deepen our understanding of our Latter-day Passover.

The first chapter of John describes John the Baptist looking at Jesus and saying to those around him, "Behold the Lamb of God!" (John 1:36). From its outset, the Gospel of John ties the Master to the Passover feast. In this gospel, the Passover lamb celebrates not only Israel's past redemption from Egypt but also its future redemption in a Messiah. His

blood would be a protection from darkness and death. John the Baptist, the last of the Old Testament prophets, was the first to publicly declare who that Lamb would be.

The miracle of turning the water into wine in John 2 marks the beginning of Christ's ministry. Symbolically, the water could be thought of as the Old Testament, the old covenant, and the new wine could represent the New Covenant ushered in through His ministry, death, and Resurrection. The cup of wine is mentioned specifically in the Savior's Last Supper. Traditionally, the four cups of wine of the Passover represented the four-fold promise from Jehovah made in Exodus 6:6–7: "Wherefore say unto the children of Israel, I am the Lord, and *I will bring you out* from under the burdens of the Egyptians, and *I will rid you out of their bondage*, and *I will redeem you* with a stretched out arm, and with great judgments: And *I will take you to me for a people*, and I will be to you a God" (emphases added). The Savior's Atonement offers us similar promises. He brings us out from under our burdens, He rids us of the bondage of sin, His Atonement

He brings us out from under our burdens, He rids us of the bondage of sin, His Atonement redeems us, and we become His children, His people.

redeems us, and we become His children, His people.

Continuing this Passover imagery, the Gospel of John is the only gospel that records Jesus's Bread of Life sermon given the day following the miracle of the five loaves and two fish (John 6). Jesus describes Himself as "true bread from heaven" (John 6:32) and "living bread" (John 6:51), which "a man may eat thereof, and not die" (John 6:50). When some in the audience bristled and argued over these descriptions, Jesus answered, "Except ye eat the flesh of the Son of man, and drink his blood, ye have no life in you" (John 6:53). John, writing from a time when the Passover had been changed, could now look back on the Savior's ministry and see He had been preparing for this event all along.

The Savior's last meal was Passover. We call it the Last Supper not only because it was his last meal before His Atonement but also because it was the last Passover meal as it had been historically practiced. The Lord changed Passover into sacrament with just a few short comments. Instead of talking

THE BREAD OF LIFE

Luke 22:19

This piece brings me back to the first time I partook of the emblems of Christ's sacrifice.

It was in a small rented room on top of a soccer stadium in Sofia, Bulgaria. A picture of Christ was taped to one of the walls, and a table, half a dozen missionaries, and a couple of investigators, including myself, filled the room.

Because multiple religions had flooded the country following the fall of the Berlin Wall, I had visited many services among many different faiths and congregations.

Somehow, though, in this small and simple space, as I thought of Christ during that first sacrament service, I felt a sense of coming home, of belonging and knowing that I was loved in a way I had never known before. It was the closest thing I had ever felt to the love of my family, yet it took that love and enhanced, broadened, and extended it far beyond what I had imagined possible. What a gift that experience was. What a gift each subsequent sacrament has been—to be with the Savior, to come to know Him, and to feel that most wonderful of all love.

about remembering Moses and Pharaoh, the plagues, or the Red Sea, the Lord told his disciples the bread of the meal would be "in remembrance of my body; for as oft as ye do this ye will remember this hour that I was with you" (Joseph Smith Translation, Mark 14:21). As they drank the wine, He told them, "This is in remembrance of my blood which is shed for many, and the new testament which I give unto you" (Joseph Smith Translation, Mark 14:23). The bread and wine would henceforth be an ordinance to remember Him and His ministry (see Joseph Smith Translation, Mark 14:20–26).

Following the meal, He and his disciples sang together. Then came the long walk to Gethsemane.

The Jews of Jesus's day loved Passover. They taught their children about it. The time they spent in preparation made it special. How careful and present they were in such important moments made it holy. The symbols of their redemption from darkness and death filled them with joy.

Today, the Savior has asked us to participate in our Latter-day Passover every week. What a blessing! Frequency and familiarity don't have to become complacency and carelessness. No matter how you've treated the sacrament in the past, your next experience with this ordinance can be the very best of your life. Do you see the sacrament as our Passover? How special is it to you? How holy is it to you? Do you prepare for it? Are we careful and present during those brief moments of prayer and meditation that comprise the sacrament?

When you sing the sacrament hymns, remember the Savior and his disciples singing together before walking to Gethsemane. When the bread is being torn to pieces, remember the Savior's flesh being torn by the crown or by the nails in his hands and feet. When putting the water to your lips or hearing the sacrament cups dropping individually into the trays, remember His blood, remember His suffering, remember the price for your peace was upon Him.

"I WAS WITH YOU."

AS A LITTLE CHILD

Matthew 18:2–5

At some point in our young lives, we all go through a change. I'm not talking about the change to your body that you learned about in your fifth-grade health class. I'm talking about a change in your mind and your heart that begins at a very young age. Recently, I noticed this change beginning to happen for my six-year-old daughter, Taylor.

I had just put the kids to bed and was putting away laundry in my room when Taylor got up from the bedroom she shares with her brother Oliver, walked in, and asked, "Mom, am I skinny?"

I stopped and looked down at her face in an attempt to read where this question was coming from. She looked a bit worried. "You're perfect," I replied.

"Okay, but am I skinny, or am I normal? Because Oliver said he thinks I'm skinny but that I might be normal. He's not sure."

"Normal," I said. "You're definitely normal."

Taylor seemed satisfied with this response and went back to bed. She felt better. But not me. I felt a little sad now, as I realized she was beginning to change. She was becoming aware that people have ideas about what bodies should be like. Soon she'll realize their opinions go far beyond bodies. Along with this will come the realization that things don't always go according to plan, that people can be disappointing, and that disasters happen in the world every single day. She'll worry about this. She'll have opinions and ideas of her own, and she'll wrestle with what's real, what's true, and how to navigate the world given the chaos that this life can be. She'll wake up from the dream life I've tried so hard to create for her, and while the experts call this "growing up" and suggest that it is healthy and normal, my momma heart breaks every time I notice the fading away of a part of life that feels a bit like magic.

In Matthew 18:2–5 we are taught that to enter into the kingdom of heaven, we must become like a child. I don't know about you, but I am very comforted by this commandment because I am childlike in so many ways. For example, I prefer refined sugar over fruits and vegetables. I watch too much TV and feel as though I should get to buy something in any store I go into. I don't like to be told what to do, and I might even respond with, "You're not the boss of me," from time to time. But, of course, this is not what the Lord means when He directs us to become as a little child. What He means is to return to the magic.

It's not *actually* magic, but when I am successful at letting go of trying to control the world, humbling myself, and just believing that everything is fine because God is in charge, it feels magical. Returning to the magic of childhood is letting go of fear and stepping into faith. It's choosing to believe even when there seems to be no evidence to support it. It's loving people who don't even like us. It's releasing the worry that feels so important and relaxing into the peace that is our birthright as children of divine lineage. And it's extremely challenging

> Returning to the magic of childhood is letting go of fear and stepping into faith. It's choosing to believe even when there seems to be no evidence to support it.

to do because of how our heavenly parents created us.

When we are born, our brains are not fully developed. In fact, the prefrontal cortex, which is the part of the brain responsible for logic, reason, long-term planning, and complex problem-solving, does not fully mature until we are twenty-four years old.[1] Taylor's prefrontal cortex is already beginning to grow. This is the awakening. This is the change. This is why the innocence and faith that comes naturally to us as children requires more consciousness as we get older.

Now, having a mature prefrontal cortex is extremely valuable. It also doesn't exist in any other animal the way it does for us

---

1 "Content: Brain Maturation Is Complete at about 24 Years of Age," *The Alcohol Pharmacology Education Partnership*, https://sites.duke.edu/apep/module-3-alcohol-cell-suicide-and-the-adolescent-brain/content-brain-maturation-is-complete-at-about-24-years-of-age.

humans. It's the reason I can create a better life for myself and my family than my French bulldog Finn will ever be able to create on his own for himself. Finn lacks the ability to think about what he wants next year. He thinks only about what he wants right now, which is always food. He also lacks the ability to solve complex problems. So these smarty-pants brains of mine and yours mean we are blessed and will get to have a complex and dynamic life experience as a result. But if we truly desire to enter into the kingdom of heaven in this life and the next, we must keep this part of us in check. Because this part of the brain wants everything to make sense. It wants things that are true to be

provable. It wants to know how. How does it work? How is it that Christ's sacrifice for us makes up for what we are incapable of doing for ourselves? How will we be judged in a way that is fair to all given the unfairness of our life circumstances? How can there be a God when there is so much suffering in the world? You get the idea. These questions are unanswerable. Sometimes we can't possibly know how. And once we're changed in the way mature brains change us, the prefrontal cortex hates unanswered questions. It wants to stomp its feet and say, "If you can't prove it, then it can't be real. I'm no fool." But the truth is that when we let go of needing it all to make sense and choose to follow what feels expansive and loving, then we get to live a life that is filled with less pain and fear. When we trust and believe and live according to that belief, we create a life that is instead filled with moments of unreasonable joy as the prefrontal cortex settles down and we reconnect with the child within us. I'm not always good at doing this, but at times I do connect with the child within me and give myself permission to believe things that I can't explain to my prefrontal brain.

I believe my daughter Taylor is right on track and will have the exact life she's meant

WE CREATE A LIFE THAT IS INSTEAD FILLED WITH MOMENTS OF UNREASONABLE JOY.

to have. I choose to believe that I'm going to die right on time. I believe people are doing their best even when their best is pretty bad. And I believe we are all loved fiercely by heavenly parents who sent Their Son. I believe that because of the Atonement of that Son, who is Jesus Christ, all the messiness of this life will return to peace and calm and order in the end.

A few years ago, my mother underwent chemotherapy to treat the cancer in her body. The effects of the chemo on her mental and emotional health were frightening. She was in excruciating pain for longer than anyone should be asked to endure. At the time I was teaching the nine-year-old Primary class at church, and Lilah was one of the children in my class. She is one of the sweetest spirits I've ever known, with her big eyes and soft voice. From time to time I mentioned my mother and her trial when it seemed appropriate to help illustrate a principle or connect with the children. One day, Lilah's older sister was at our house visiting with my daughter, and she shared that sometimes when they say family prayers, they give everyone in the family an opportunity to share what they'd like everyone else to pray for on their behalf. I thought this was a lovely tradition. Then Lilah's sister went on to explain that the previous evening when it was Lilah's turn to share, she'd said, "I'd like everyone to please pray for Sister Moore's mom."

This is what becoming as a little child looks like. This is the faith, humility, and self-lessness of a child. This is the state that gets us to the kingdom of heaven in this life and the next.

FOR THE LOVE
OF ONE

Matthew 18:11–14

On our small home farm, my daughter has a lot of animals (upwards of a hundred). I can't tell two sister sheep, Faith and Charity, apart from one another, and there's no way I would ever know if a hen went missing. My daughter, on the other hand, knows them by name, and she can tell if they aren't themselves that day or if one has been separated from the flock.

Watching her, I appreciate more than I otherwise might that the Savior knows us just as well and is willing to go into the wilderness to find us and bring us home. I often feel like that's precisely what He did in preparing me to receive the gospel and sending missionaries to find me as a teenager in Bulgaria. I was nobody of significance, but He knew me; He went out of His way to find me and bring me to Him.

AS I HAVE LOVED YOU

John 13:3–16, 34

I remember the day I caught a glimpse of a truth that changed me completely. Or, at least, I remember certain parts of that day. Other things I don't remember at all. For example, I don't remember what time of year it was. This is probably because I was living in Orange County, California, where the weather doesn't change much and every day is nothing short of gorgeous. I don't remember exactly how old I was or even who my roommates were at the time. But what I do remember is the feeling I felt as I entered my bishop's office and the very, very different feeling I felt after I left.

I was a young single adult the first time I went to a bishop to receive guidance through the repentance process, not because I had never made a mistake that warranted the help of a Church leader but because I had not been able to muster up the courage to do so before.

Admitting you've gone wrong is tough. Doing so out loud to someone in authority you don't know very well is downright humiliating. Or so I thought.

I remember sitting in the hallway outside his door, waiting for my turn to talk to the bishop. I wasn't sure if I wanted the time to speed up or slow down. I wasn't sure how to say what I needed to say, and I was nervous and afraid. When it was my turn, the bishop smiled, welcomed me into his office, and invited me to sit down. I couldn't look him in the eye as I started explaining to him why I was there. I sobbed as I shared with him where I'd taken a turn in my life that wasn't leading me to where I wanted to go. I wasn't sure how much detail I was supposed to give. I looked to him for guidance and waited to see what sort of interrogating questions he would ask. He asked very few. He mostly listened.

After a few minutes of unloading my thoughts, I shrugged my shoulders in confusion about what to do or say next and kept my head down in preparation for the lecture I knew was to follow. I knew he would tell me I had made some serious mistakes. That these were things the Lord doesn't take lightly. That I needed to feel godly sorrow in order to be forgiven and that I must now suffer the consequences of my mistakes. I knew that part was coming. So I sat in that chair in that small office and braced myself. But the most unexpected thing happened next.

My bishop didn't say a word until I looked up and he saw that he had my attention. I read heartache in the expression on his face. I interpreted it as his feeling sorry for me because of what a mess I'd made, but it wasn't that at all. As he spoke, he said, "Jody, you are confused about how your Heavenly Father feels about you. He loves you more immensely than you can imagine."

I nodded in agreement. I'd been taught that my heavenly parents love me, and yes, I knew that. But I was under the impression that

HE LOVES YOU MORE IMMENSELY THAN YOU CAN IMAGINE.

They love me a little bit less when I sin. That They are disappointed and frustrated with me in these moments.

The bishop explained to me that I was wrong. "Tell me about someone you love. Someone you are close to," he said.

I told him about my younger sister Natalie, who lived in New York City at the time. She was struggling with some of her own trials, and I missed her terribly and wished I could live closer to her, hang out with her, connect

with her, and help her. The bishop then asked me to imagine Natalie had done what I had done and was sitting in a chair telling me what I had just told him. He asked me if I would love her any less than I usually do.

"No," I replied quickly and easily.

He went on to remind me that the love I have for my little sister is only a tiny fraction of the love God has for us.

The book of John in the New Testament contains one of the most famous verses of scripture of all time. It's commonly recited in Christian churches across the globe, especially at Christmas and Easter. It's secretly printed on the underside of the cup at some of your favorite fast-food joints, and it is even displayed with pride on cardboard signage in NFL crowds. John 3:16 reads, "For God so loved the world, that he gave his only begotten Son, that whosoever believeth in him should not perish, but have everlasting life."

Did you hear that? Everlasting life. On the surface, when we think of everlasting life, we think of a never-ending existence that is available to all men and women born on Earth; I believe that is a component of it, but it is more than just eternal existence. Everlasting life is about the opportunity we have to live a truly joy-filled existence in our earthly life and in the eternities, and this is available because of God's love and the sacrifice made by His Son Jesus Christ.

Elder Joseph B. Wirthlin said, "The just as well as the unjust are given a priceless and incomprehensible gift: immortality. Because of Jesus the Christ, we will live forever. We are immortal. Eternal life, however, is something altogether different. Immortality is about quantity. Eternal life is about quality."[1]

God's unwavering love for us is not only a comforting thing to remember when we're feeling down. His love and the sacrifice made by His Son mean that we can experience peace, love, and immeasurable joy now and forever. My wise and loving California bishop understood this and offered it to me that day in his office as he had me think about my sister Natalie. As I did so, I stopped feeling the shame and embarrassment I'd been feeling and instead felt an immense fullness of love for my sister—a tiny glimpse into what our heavenly parents feel for us.

This love is not reserved for the righteous. It is not just for the people succeeding in some way. It is not given more fully to us when we have one of those days on which we read our scriptures, have patience instead of yelling at the kids, and get caught up on the laundry. Our heavenly parents' love is full and complete, and there is nothing we can do that will change that. And it is for every one of us. Amazing!

I don't expect I will ever fully comprehend this truth in this lifetime, but I will never stop trying. Because when we understand that every single person born on Earth (including ourselves) is loved completely and fully, everything changes. Everything. We can stop blaming others and shaming ourselves. We can stop looking for good guys and bad guys. We can let go of judgment and instead be curious. We can

> God's unwavering love for us is not only a comforting thing to remember when we're feeling down. His love and the sacrifice made by His Son mean that we can experience peace, love, and immeasurable joy now and forever.

---

1   Joseph B. Wirthlin, "Timely Topics: What Is the Difference between Immortality and Eternal Life?," *New Era*, November 2006, 8.

remember that being a human is tough and we will all fall short at times, but we can also remember that because of God's perfect love and Christ's atoning sacrifice, we can choose to get up again and strive to live with love.

RACING TO AN EMPTY TOMB

John 20:2–4

This piece speaks joy to me. Had we been there after two long nights of mourning, I wonder how fast we would have run, filled with the anticipation of discovering that all was not lost, that He had risen, that God prevailed then, that He prevails always, and that hope endures because of Christ.

Each Easter morning brings another chance for us to relive that most wonderful of moments and bask in that joy.

DID NOT OUR HEART BURN

Luke 24:13–32

One spring day, as I was cheering on my son at his soccer game, I saw a mom beeline toward me. You have had that happen, haven't you? You see a stranger marching toward you, and you know she will be angry—but she is a stranger! Why is she heading your way? Well, she stomped up, put a hand on her hip, and said, "You teach religion at BYU, don't you?" I usually know where the rest of a conversation is going when it starts this way. I really just wanted to continue watching the game, but of course, I answered, "Yes, I do." She said, "Well, if the Church were true, wouldn't it be bigger?"

"What do you mean?" I asked.

She jumped right in. "Really, if the Church were true, it would be bigger, wouldn't it?"

I wasn't sarcastic but honestly asked her, "Why do you think that? What makes you an expert on true churches? How do you know how big they are supposed to be?"

She thought about it for a second and then said, "Okay, I just thought it would be bigger. I just *assumed* it would be."

Through experiences like this one, I've found that there are times when my assumptions, not the Church or the gospel, are the problem. If we want to conquer our concerns, we have to check our assumptions and examine our expectations before we doubt the Church or even God. We are in good company, though, when we make assumptions about the Savior.

In Luke 24, we meet two men walking. The story begins in verse 13. On the Sunday of Jesus's Resurrection, two people are walking from Jerusalem to a village named Emmaus. Emmaus is said to be "about threescore furlongs" (verse 13), which is about 7.5 miles or 12 kilometers. Jerusalem is on a hill, and the area is steep, so the distance would have taken a few hours to travel, even for people accustomed to walking long distances.

One man is named Cleopas, and the other remains unnamed. They know Jesus has been arrested and killed and that the tomb is empty, and as they walk, the two men talk.

Tradition tells us that Cleopas was Joseph the carpenter's brother, though the scriptures don't confirm this. Jesus would have known his uncle. His uncle would have known Jesus—His story, what He looked like. Hegesippus, a second-century author, suggests that Cleopas was a family member of Mary, Jesus's mother. Others also added details in later centuries—I don't know if they are true, but I like to think they make the stories more meaningful and personal.

Luke tells us that

they talked together of all these things which had happened. And it came to pass, that, while they communed together and reasoned, Jesus himself drew near, and went with them. But their eyes were holden that they should not know him. And he said unto them, What manner of communications are these that ye have one to another, as ye walk, and are sad? And the one of them, whose name was Cleopas answering said unto him, Art thou only a stranger in Jerusalem, and has not known the things which are come to pass there in these days? And he said unto them, What things? And they said unto him, Concerning Jesus of Nazareth, which was a prophet mighty in deed and word before God and all the people: And now the chief priests and our rulers delivered him to be condemned to death, and have crucified him. But we trusted that it had been he which should have redeemed Israel: And beside all this, to day is the third day since these things were done. (Luke 24:14–21)

Imagine the scene. You and your family and friends have been under Roman rule. Life hasn't been easy nor completely free from brutality and despotism. You pray and yearn for Israel's redemption from Rome. You have hoped and prayed for the Promised One to come and free you. Jesus has been born and is performing miracles. All of your hopes rest on Him to save you. But it doesn't

happen the way you imagined it would. He is tried and killed in the most humiliating and brutal of ways. It has been three days. You are walking to Emmaus from Jerusalem, heavy with grief and disappointment. You and your friend discuss how you had thought Jesus would be the one to save you from Roman rule. You had assumed Jesus would do things in a certain way. It didn't happen. Saddened and confused, you and your friend are discussing what has happened, when a man walks up and asks,

"What are you talking about, and why are you both so sad?"

Cleopas seems incredulous. Is this guy kidding? Where has he been if he hasn't heard about Jesus, His trial, and His Crucifixion?

Under a rock? Cleopas asks him if he is a stranger in town if he hasn't heard the things that have transpired. The man asks, "What things?" Cleopas and his friend explain about Jesus of Nazareth. Jesus is a prophet and has accomplished great deeds, but He died, they say. They tell the man that the women went to the sepulchre that morning and Jesus's body is gone, and the women had seen angels telling them Jesus was alive. And then comes the part I want you to notice. They say, "But we trusted that it had been he which should have redeemed Israel" (Luke 24:21).

And, of course, the man is Jesus (but they don't recognize Him), and He says, "O fools, and slow of heart to believe all that the prophets have spoken" (verse 25). And then

He starts fixing their assumptions. He goes back through the scriptures beginning at Moses—that is, Genesis—and teaches them about Himself. He teaches them for hours as they walk.

When they arrive at their home, Jesus (who they still don't recognize) is going to leave, and they say, "No, no, no, stay here. Stay here; stay with us." So He breaks bread with them and blesses it. And, at that moment, they figure out who He is, and He vanishes.

My favorite is what they say when He's gone. "Did not our heart burn within us, while He talked with us by the way, and while he opened to us the scriptures?" (verse 32).

Now I want you to find a way to apply this story to your life. Can you do that for me? Maybe this story from my friend (used with permission) can help:

I had an idea of how my life would go. It would be picture-perfect. I could almost imagine it, like a montage or slideshow. I imagined I would meet my spouse at BYU; we would have children, raise them in the Church, and struggle, but those times would strengthen us. We would laugh about the nights we ate bean soup again or had to glue Cub Scout badges on our son's shirt because neither of us sews. We would struggle but laugh, serve in our ward, and watch our children grow up together. The only part of that that happened was my not being able to sew the badges on the Cub Scout uniform (can you say glue gun?). One of our daughters reminds me that someone had her quit Daisies because they couldn't sew one more flower petal on her Girl Scout uniform. That sort of sounds like me. Okay, it was me.

I thought my "rough around the edges" and "heart of gold" spouse would grow up and become a family man. I imagined our life would be full of great memories. I could already imagine our family photos. I thought we would watch our children's progress in Young Men and Young Women. I thought we would attend their sporting events and parent-teacher nights and enjoy them growing up in our local ward. As the years passed, however, I served alone. I realized I was wrong. I was very wrong. One day, he left me and the kids crying and drove away. He had packed his car and had a new apartment. He left us.

I never expected to add this to our family story. I had assumed things would be very different.

After he left, I felt abandoned—by my husband and by God. The nights stretched on forever, and although friends and family were generous and kind, the heavens seemed closed. I had prayed for all twenty-five years of marriage. I had fasted. I had accepted every calling, but my spouse had walked further and further away. He told me he could love me if. If I would drink or do drugs. If I would quit serving in seminary. If I stopped believing in and attending church. If I stopped wearing my temple garments. If I stopped believing in Jesus.

I couldn't deny the truth, nor who I was. The Lord had blessed me in such obvious and powerful ways throughout my life. I couldn't deny my testimony, but being abandoned by a spouse was more painful than I could have imagined. I'd thought I might experience persecution for my beliefs, but I'd never imagined it from the man who had promised to take care of me.

I remember my sophomore year of seminary. When we were taught about the early members of the Church being persecuted and dying for their faith, I remember thinking, "I would do that! I would die for the Savior—bring it on!" I was naive and ridiculous. I had no idea the person I loved most would be the one who asked me to choose between him and the Lord.

I felt my prayers had gone unheard. I attended the temple. I prayed some more. After my husband left, I felt more alone, and the pain was too heavy to carry. The days and nights went on, and there were many days I struggled to get out of bed. I was overwhelmed. Why wouldn't God answer my prayers? Why had He forsaken me?

The days and months passed, and improvement was agonizingly slow. Mental health care, physical care, blessings, service, work, and love all helped me slowly return to my former happy self. It took years, and to be honest, there are still days I must work to achieve happiness.

One morning, as I taught my early-morning seminary class, one young woman asked me a question I had never heard nor thought of before. She asked me if I found a common theme when reading the Gospels that year. Did I find various applications each year that I studied, or did I tend to see the same things? This was a great question. I didn't have a great answer—at least, not right

"The Lord had blessed me in such obvious and powerful ways throughout my life."

away. That night, however, as I flipped through the pages of my scriptures, I saw the answer quite clearly. I had written the same types of thing in the margins of my scriptures, over and over. "Jesus is with us. Jesus is with them. Jesus never leaves us alone." To me, personally, this message was the most powerful in the story of Jesus appearing on the road to Emmaus. Let me explain.

Although there are many excellent applications, that night, this story resonated for me as no other story had previously. It was my long-awaited answer for help. You see, Jesus walks with the disciples, but they don't recognize Him. They had assumed things would be different—that it would go differently. The disciples were like me. I had thought things would go differently. These disciples said, "But we trusted that it had been he which should have redeemed [us]" (Luke 24:21). They were disappointed, confused, and disoriented. I had trusted that my life would go a certain way. I had also assumed and trusted. And, just as He did for those men as they traveled on their path, the Savior opens the scriptures to us and shows us that He has been here all along. "Beginning at Moses and all the prophets [from the beginning of the Bible to every prophet], he

expounded unto them in all the scriptures the things concerning himself" (verse 27). They didn't recognize his mission in Israel; they had wanted a different sort of Savior. I saw myself as those men. I wanted something different from what the Lord had promised and given me. I didn't see Him. I expected different blessings in my life, but I missed the tremendous gifts the Lord was giving. Like those disciples, I couldn't always see Jesus because I expected and wanted something different— something less than He provided.

And just like the disciples, when "their eyes were opened, and they knew him" (verse 31), I could almost feel the Savior, His hand on my shoulder as we looked back at the slideshow of my life and He showed me that He had been there, guiding, encouraging, and blessing me. I could see the three children I have and how the ward members had helped raise them. I saw the good friends the Lord had put into my path. I saw the many opportunities to serve that had taught me so many lessons I couldn't have learned in other ways. I saw the hours I'd helped not only at various schools and jobs but at the temple. I had been blessed every single day. The pictures came into focus, and I could see that He had always been there. He had always been with me.

He wasn't the Savior I had expected but was One so much more powerful, so much more personal, and so much more significant. Sister Michelle D. Craig said, "Trust God to lead you even if that way looks different than you expected or is different from others" (Michelle D. Craig, "Spiritual Capacity," Ensign, *November 2019, 21).*

The Savior has given me the job of my dreams, great friendships, a calling, and a renewed sense of purpose. He has helped me turn the ashes of my marriage into a life that I love— one I would have never had the courage to create without my spouse leaving that day. Now I have the opportunity to have in my home art depicting the Savior, the freedom to indulge my habit of collecting Church books, and the privilege to openly live the gospel of Jesus Christ.

I believe this will be true of my entire life. One day, the Savior will sit by my side as we look back through my life, and He will come into focus, just as He did for Cleopas and the other disciple, for He has been there all along.

When things don't go the way you thought they should have gone, ask God to show you

"Be assured that the ending of the book of our lives will exceed our grandest expectations."

His plans. The Savior gently corrects our expectations or assumptions. He doesn't only save us from our current problems in the manner we often would like or assume would be the best way, like the Israelites, who wanted to be rescued from Rome's cruel rule. Jesus Christ frees us from sin and pain and death. He does so much more than we can comprehend. As President Dieter F. Uchtdorf said, "No matter how bleak the chapter of our lives may look today, because of the life and sacrifice of Jesus Christ, we may hope and be assured that the ending of the book of our lives will exceed our grandest expectations."[1]

When it comes to Jesus, expect the unexpected.

---

1 Dieter F. Uchtdorf, "The Infinite Power of Hope," *Ensign*, November 2008, 22.

MY LORD
AND MY GOD

John 20:24–29

In my study of scripture, I am often amazed at how we can know a story so well, yet when we return to it with an open heart, it's as if additional light suddenly illuminates the story in a whole new way.

I had that experience when creating this piece depicting Thomas holding the Savior's resurrected hand.

This story, I think, isn't so much a sermon on doubting. Many of the Apostles questioned the possibility of their Lord's Resurrection only to understand fully once they had beheld him again. It's easy to say Thomas should have just taken the rest of the Apostles' word for it, but he really wanted to see for himself the risen Christ and feel the prints in His hands.

The fact that Christ then appeared specifically to Thomas, answering this heartfelt plea, shows so much of that individual grace and love He shares for each of us.

The admonition to be not faithless but believing is a powerful one. We all have questions, but through all we don't yet know, all we haven't yet seen, we can learn to trust in the goodness we have seen, the love we have felt, and the joy we have known so far. We can also know of a surety that God's hand will help us and continue to guide us even when we cannot see and do not yet understand all He has in store for us.

HOW BEAUTIFUL UPON THE MOUNTAINS

Isaiah 52:7–10

This is one of the more adventurous pieces I have undertaken, mostly because it involved a very steep hike up the face of a mountain. Yes, there are some stone stairs, but they might as well be ladder rungs since you can see almost straight down when looking back (something I tried not to do very often). With the encouragement of my kids, I eventually reached the summit, where a swarm of mosquitoes waited patiently to ambush us.

Still undaunted, we proceeded with the shoot. That's when the miracle happened. The sky, which had been threatening to rain for an hour, opened up for a window of about fifteen minutes with these magnificent Michelangelo clouds, and it made for the perfect background. There is also some wonderful symbolism involved in the location. The flat area at the summit is called Table Rock, and it has this big split down the middle of it, just like the stone table that symbolized Christ's Atonement in The Lion, the Witch, and the Wardrobe.

ANTHONY SWEAT

ENCIRCLED IN THE ARMS OF HIS LOVE

2 Nephi 1:15

Near the end of his life, the prophet Lehi gave a patriarchal plea for his spiritually wayward sons, Laman and Lemuel. Lehi prophesied to them and promised blessings for them. He invited, warned, and rebuked, even resorting to saying, in essence, "Wake up and man up!" (see 2 Nephi 1:21, 23). He used words like "trembling," "anxiety," and "weighed down" to describe his worries about them (2 Nephi 1:14, 16–17). How many of us as parents, friends, ministers, or leaders can relate when we reflect on the spiritual wanderings of those we love? Although Lehi says much in this chapter of possible solutions, he uttered a line I believe is a key teaching for those who struggle and for those who want to help: "I have beheld [God's] glory, and I am encircled about eternally in the arms of his love" (verse 15). The answer, like it always is, is charity.

Charity is a small English word that encompasses a large heavenly concept. Originally the word was *agape*, which is Greek for "the fatherly love of God for humans and their reciprocal love for God."[1] Charity is different than romantic or friendly or familial love. It surely is much, much more than doing kind acts of service for others (as important as those are). Charity is a spiritual gift from heaven that occurs when you grasp glimpses of the grandeur of the work and glory of God and are encircled by his indescribable love for His children. "And again, I remember that thou hast said that thou [Jesus] hast loved the world, even unto the laying down of thy life for the world . . . And now I know that this love which thou

---

1 Seslisözlük, "agape," seslisozluk.net/en/what-is-the-meaning-of-agape./

hast had for the children of men is charity" (Ether 12:33–34). Charity is not only about God loving us, however, but also our loving Him in return. "We love him, because he first loved us" (1 John 4:19), John taught.

CHARITY IS WHEN, AS A GIFT FROM HEAVEN, GOD SAYS, "I LOVE YOU."

Charity is when, as a gift from heaven, God says, "I love you," and out of experiencing that divine love, our natural reply to God is, "I love you too." Charity is something we receive, not give. Charity is not what we do to others; it's about what God does to us.

In the words of President Dallin H. Oaks, "charity . . . is not an *act* but a *condition* or state of being."[2]

Lehi knows this because he has experienced this state of being. To better understand, let's go back a few chapters to Lehi's dream, found in 1 Nephi 8, and Nephi's visionary interpretation of the dream in 1 Nephi 11–14. In his dream, or vision, Lehi sees a glorious tree with exquisite white fruit. He approaches the tree and eats of the fruit, and it fills his soul. After this heavenly experience, Lehi says, "I began to be desirous that my family should partake of it also; for I knew that it was desirable above all other fruit" (1 Nephi 8:12). Seeking to understand and know for himself the meaning and truth of his father's vision, Lehi's son Nephi later has a vision also and sees a similar tree, desiring to know its meaning. In answer, an angel shows him a future vision of Jesus being born on Earth (see 1 Nephi 11:18–20). The angel then asks, "Knowest thou the meaning of the tree which thy

2   Dallin H. Oaks, "The Challenge to Become," *Ensign*, November 2000.

father saw?" (verse 21) and Nephi responds affirmatively, "Yea, it is the love of God, which sheddeth itself abroad in the hearts of the children of men; wherefore, it is the most desirable above all things" (verse 22), which links Nephi's understanding to Lehi's description that the fruit was "desirable above all other fruit" (1 Nephi 8:12).

God's love—manifest most thoroughly in the life, person, teachings, and sacrifice of Jesus Christ—is charity. We aren't accustomed to talking about the fruit of the tree of life this way, but when Lehi ate the fruit, he ate charity. He tasted the love of God, and that love profoundly affected him, as it does all those who savor the Savior. It is interesting to link the love of God with something you taste, like fruit or food. The Book of Mormon does this a few other times. Jacob tells his people to "feast upon [God's] love" (Jacob 3:2). King Benjamin says his people "have known of [God's] goodness and have tasted of his love . . . which causeth such exceedingly great joy in your souls" (Mosiah 4:11). After Alma the Younger is born of God through his experience with Christ, he later says he wanted others to "taste of the exceeding joy of which I did taste" (Alma 36:24). Mormon says of an experience he had when he was young, "I was visited of the Lord, and tasted and knew of the goodness of Jesus" (Mormon 1:15). In the New Testament, the author of

Hebrews talks about those who "have tasted of the heavenly gift . . . and have tasted the good word of God, and the powers of the world to come" (Hebrews 6:4–5).

Why is tasting this greatest heavenly gift of charity (see 1 Nephi 15:36) the answer—for those who struggle and those who serve? Mormon says, "Wherefore, cleave unto charity, which is the greatest of all" (Moroni 7:46). Paul says we can have and do and try most everything else—for us, this might include great ward activities, reason, data, ministering, family get-togethers, titles, sermons, and whatever else—but if we don't have charity, we and it are nothing (see 1 Corinthians 13:1–3). Why? Back to Lehi's experience in his dream, there are at least two reasons:

1: Charity fills us with true, lasting joy. We each hunger for essential things in this life: love, peace, self-worth, respect, companionship, purpose, recognition, belonging. We seek to fill those hungers through various ways and sometimes in the wrong way (out of ignorance or rebellion). How many problems in life have been the result of misguided attempts to fill a deep and unmet need! Perhaps one of the greatest hungers we each deeply desire is lasting happiness. The love of God, or charity, is the only real long-term answer for relieving this hunger. Lehi says, "As I partook of the fruit thereof it filled my soul with exceedingly great joy" (1 Nephi 8:12). Not just joy, but *exceedingly great* joy! Nephi explained of his vision, "The love of God . . . is the most desirable above all things." The angel quickly added, "and the most joyous to the soul" (1 Nephi 11:22–23). When deep hungers are met, the aroma of sin often ceases. Wickedness loses its attractiveness when we experience inner happiness.

2. Charity fills us with a love of others. After Lehi ate of the fruit, notice how he immediately began to think of his family, turned toward them, and was desirous that they should partake also (see 1 Nephi 8:12). Experiencing the love of God causes us to turn outward and love others more like God. The Prophet Joseph Smith taught, "Love is one of the leading characteristics of Deity, and ou[gh]t to be manifested by those who aspire to be the Sons of God. A man filled with the love of God, is not content with blessing his family alone, but ranges through the world, anxious to bless the whole of the human family."[3] President Dieter F. Uchtdorf taught, "When our hearts

In a simple gospel equation, God's love for us + our love for God = loving others more like God.

are filled with the love of God, something good and pure happens to us . . . the easier it is to love others with the pure love of Christ. As we open our hearts to the glowing dawn of the love of God, the darkness and cold of animosity and envy will eventually fade."[4] In a simple gospel equation, *God's love for us + our love for God = loving others more like God.*

Lehi knew if he could just get his wayward sons to taste the glory and love of God, it could solve the problems he foresaw. If they could remain in those encircled arms of the Holy One, charity would fill them with love and joy and change them to joyfully love others. Charity was the answer for them, and it is the only real answer for us today, whether we are spiritual wanderers or shepherds gathering His sheep. Let us "pray unto the Father with all the energy of heart, that [we] may be filled with this love," which God promises to bestow "upon all who are true followers of his Son, Jesus Christ" (Moroni 7:48).

3   "Letter to Quorum of the Twelve, 15 December 1840," p. [2], The Joseph Smith Papers, josephsmithpapers.org/paper -summary/letter-to-quorum-of-the-twelve-15-decem- ber-1840/2

4   Dieter F. Uchtdorf, "The Merciful Obtain Mercy," *Ensign*, May 2012, 75–76.

THE FINISHER OF OUR FAITH
BY ADAM TIMOTHY

High upon Golgotha,
A hill, that all might see,
The Light of all the World
Was hung upon a tree.

The oil of redemption
Sin's awful weight did press.
The Anointed One had overcome
The world with grace to bless.

And with it each soul's lantern,
Fresh filled with what He wrought,
Shines brighter through the darkness,
Which comprehendeth not

That Holiest of Holies,
Tabernacle of a God,
Whose feet, now bruised and pierced,
A perfect path had trod.

His hands and wrists by nails made sure,
Oh Gilead's great balm,
A love sealed fast through covenant
Engraven on each palm.

Living water gave He freely,
The Last and also First,
When He drank the cup most bitter
And now was left to thirst.

The Word, the Lamb, the great I Am,
Now left to cry, "Eloi!"
Now sees His seed set there before
Salvation's crowning joy.

Then rends the veil, descends the storm;
All nature, torn, it cries,
Messiah's soul sees three days more,
Eternal, the Son rise!

JOHN BYTHEWAY

John Bytheway was born and raised in Salt Lake City, and he served his mission in the Philippines. He earned a master's degree in Religious Education from BYU and is a part-time instructor at the BYU Salt Lake Center, where he teaches courses on the Book of Mormon and the Gospels. He has served in The Church of Jesus Christ of Latter-day Saints as a Young Men's president, an executive secretary, a high councilor, and a bishop.

John and his wife, Kimberly, have six children and a completely full SUV, which doubles in value when it's full of gasoline. John currently serves as a member of the Young Men's general advisory council (formerly known as the general board). His oldest daughter, Ashley, served her mission in Lyon, France; his oldest son, Andrew, returned recently from his mission in Iceland; and his daughter Natalie is currently serving in Tahiti.

Learn more about John at johnbytheway.com, or follow him on social media.

Facebook: facebook.com/johnbytheway

AL CARRAWAY

Al Carraway is a convert to The Church of Jesus Christ of Latter-day Saints, a writer, a multi-award-winning international speaker, and author of the best-selling books *Wildly Optimistic, More Than the Tattooed Mormon, Cheers to Eternity, Finding Yourself in the New Testament* (coming October 2022), and more.

Starting in 2010, she has traveled worldwide, inspiring others with faith through difficult times. Her passion is to help everyone learn how to find and love God in the hard, the unwanted, and the unexpected. Because, through it all, with God, we have every reason to be wildly optimistic.

After a decade spent in Arizona and Utah, she is now living with her husband, Ben, and her three kids, back where she was raised, in New York.

Learn more about Al at alcarraway.com, or follow her on Instagram @alcarraway.

JODY MOORE

Jody Moore is a certified master life coach who has helped tens of thousands of people through her work. Jody brings her testimony of Christ into the work she does on mental and emotional resilience and strength. She hosts the *Better than Happy* podcast with over seventeen million downloads and is author of the book also titled *Better than Happy*. Jody has four children and lives with them and her husband of eighteen years in Spokane, Washington.

Learn more about Jody at jodymoore.com or follow her on social media.

Facebook: Facebook.com/jodymoorecoaching

Instagram: @jodymoorecoaching

HANK SMITH

Hank R. Smith grew up in St. George, Utah. He received a bachelor's degree in business administration from Dixie State University (2002), his MBA (2005) from Utah State University, and his PhD in educational leadership (2014) from Brigham Young University. His studies focused on the development of high trust educational organizations and their impact on student achievement. Before joining the religion faculty at BYU, he worked for fourteen years with Seminaries and Institutes of Religion as an instructor. He loves to teach from the scriptures, especially to the youth and young adults of the Church. He also enjoys consulting work with school districts and corporations centered on creating a high trust culture. He has addressed audiences in almost every state through seminars and keynote speaking engagements. His outside interests include marathons, history books, and hiking with his family. He and his incredible wife, Sara, are the parents of five children and reside in Mapleton, Utah.

Learn more about Hank Smith at hanksmith.com, or follow him on social media.

Facebook: facebook.com/hanksmithcds

Instagram: @hankrsmith

Twitter: @hankrsmith

ANTHONY SWEAT

Anthony Sweat is an associate professor of Church History and Doctrine at Brigham Young University. He is the author of several articles and books dealing with the teachings and history of The Church of Jesus Christ of Latter-day Saints. He is married to Cindy Sweat, and they are the parents of seven children.

Follow his work on Instagram @brotheranthonysweat or at anthonysweat.com.

EVA KOLEVA TIMOTHY

Eva Koleva Timothy grew up under the shadow of Communism in Eastern Europe. Yet, under the tutelage of her artist father, she learned to cherish the pursuit of personal passion and the freedom to view the world for its possibilities, whatever the circumstance.

She was one of the first converts to join The Church of Jesus Christ of Latter-day Saints in Bulgaria soon after the wall fell. She served a full-time mission in New York City, and her love of the gospel and of freedom are both major themes in her art.

Eva is known to possess an abundance of enthusiasm for life. She loves art for its inherent power to focus, refine, and inspire and speaks regularly on the power of nurturing creativity in our lives.

Eva's work has been exhibited by and/or collected at institutions internationally, including the Smithsonian National Museum of American History; the Museum of Fine Arts, Houston; and Oxford University.

Learn more about Eva at evatimothy.com, or follow her on social media.

Instagram: @eva_timothy

Facebook: facebook.com/evatimothy